The 5 Secrets

of

THE MATRIX

I0151226

The True Core of Self-Development

Zsa Zsa Tudos

First Edition

Published by AKIA Publishing

Copyright © *Zsa Zsa Tudos 2017*

Maps by *Andras Bereznay*

Photos and drawings by *Zsa Zsa Tudos*

Cover design by *Zsa Zsa Tudos*

www.zsazsatudos.com

AKIA is the philosophy that sets you free

I dedicate this book to fellow earthlings who has the drive to go on and seek happiness.

ACKNOWLEDGEMENT

My greatest thanks to my students who put me through difficult times with doubts, questions and arguments.

I thank life and nature for its beauties and lessons.

Content

Foreword

I first met Zsa Zsa when she interviewed me on her radio show, over 6 years ago. During that interview I came to realize that we were kindred spirits in our beliefs that everything in the world is interrelated, we are responsible for our own actions, and that nature is one of the greatest teachers. As such, I was deeply honoured to be asked to write the foreword for her book.

In my life and in my work I often see people struggling with their search for meaning. For a deeper understanding of what makes life work. For something more. In this fast paced and turbulent world, many of us are seeking answers and a way of living that brings more balance to our lives. Zsa Zsa has woven many concepts throughout these pages and made it a how-to book for those of us willing to question our lives and our belief systems, in order to raise our energetic vibration and consciousness, and thus help to raise the vibration and consciousness of the planet. The time to do this work really is now! The planet needs us now. While reading this book I was brought back to remembering the truth again and again; that the purpose of my spiritual journey of self-development is to become one with the Creator Force. And that my journey is not an isolated one. Because everything is interrelated, each time I remember and live that truth, I make the world a better place.

Interspersed throughout these pages are unique meditations, exercises, and practices to help us experience the self-development principles the author describes. I love that she approaches things holistically. There is something offered for the health of body, mind, and spirit, equating to what Zsa Zsa calls "soul health". Everything working in tandem to create balance.

This book invites us to build a bridge between the conscious and the subconscious. To bring forward the patterns that are not working in our lives, and replace them with ones that bring us peace. As Zsa Zsa says, "...peace derives from and dwells within...". Until we can make the subconscious conscious, and heal what needs to be healed, that peace within, that we all crave, will elude us.

I think a great work of art, whether it be a book, or a painting, or a photograph impacts us personally and prompts us to think and act globally. The *5 Secrets of the Matrix* did both for me. My hope is that it does the same for you.

Denise Cunningham, BA, RPC

Inspirational Speaker and Author of the #1 Best-Selling Book *Whispers of Hope: Transcending Abuse, Cancer and Divorce to Embrace Peace*

Prologue

My many years of life coaching and family - relationship therapy practice made me realize that regardless how many books one reads and how many webinars – seminars one attends, the core of the matter is missing. People try to build a rock castle on quick sand that starts running and undermines the future. Even though the time and place of a beginning is an individual decision lack of success speaks for itself.

Another false assumption is that life has separate compartments that are not in connection with each other. This belief causes quite a lot of heart ache and sadness on the path.

In this book I go back to as many beginnings as necessary in order to unveil information and show connections between events. Without this base ignorance sets in and takes away the possibility of a better future. One needs to understand the surrounding elements to be able to grasp the knowledge about the Self.

As everything is interrelated, I found it very difficult to grab a valued starting point to my account on Humanity at large. After long consideration I placed my vote on the equal legged cross as the most ancient symbol of life on Earth. It is not only the symbol of life but the essential understanding of existence.

Basically, it depicts humanity with its choices, directions, emotions and life cycles. Looking at the structure of the symbol it shows an earthling standing at a cross-road with arms wide

9

open, ready to embrace the Unknown, the Experience and Life itself. It also shows confidence in the Self and the universe, with the understanding that there are no bad or good choices really, only choices earthlings need to make to experience and learn. Choices are the machinery of existence. Without them the universe would stand still, in other word die. The equal legged cross also symbolizing the perfect harmony and understanding of the universe. The symbol stands for endless possibilities, countless missions and an abundance of experience. With its ultimate freedom the equal legged cross also represents the opposite pole of it all. It says that everything is connected to the Whole and the Whole is connected to everything. Every individual path runs towards the centre to contribute to the newly gained experience and knowledge, where it will be redistributed.

The equal legged cross is equality. It represents the idea that regardless of size and nature the influence of all energy is important. We are going to talk about energies in the universe at a later stage.

The four legs of the cross represent the 4 phases of earthly living – childhood, adolescence, adulthood and old age. These stations only apply to the state of the physical body rather than achievements or way of thinking. They are the 4 stations of the yearly cycle – 2 equinoxes and 2 solstices; the 4 basic elements – earth, water, air and fire; the 4 weekly cycles of the moon; the 4 initiations – Hylic, Psychic, Pneumatic and Gnostic, and the 4 directions. These are all individual cycles but they are also milestones of a greater cycle. Let us just look at the 4 initiations. The first degree is to understand earth as an element and its effect on earthlings. Here we would talk about the strong attachments to the planet. Since we live in a physical body it is natural that our centre of gravity be connected to the core of the planet. However, it also represents the strong attachment to the material itself. It is the Hylic road.

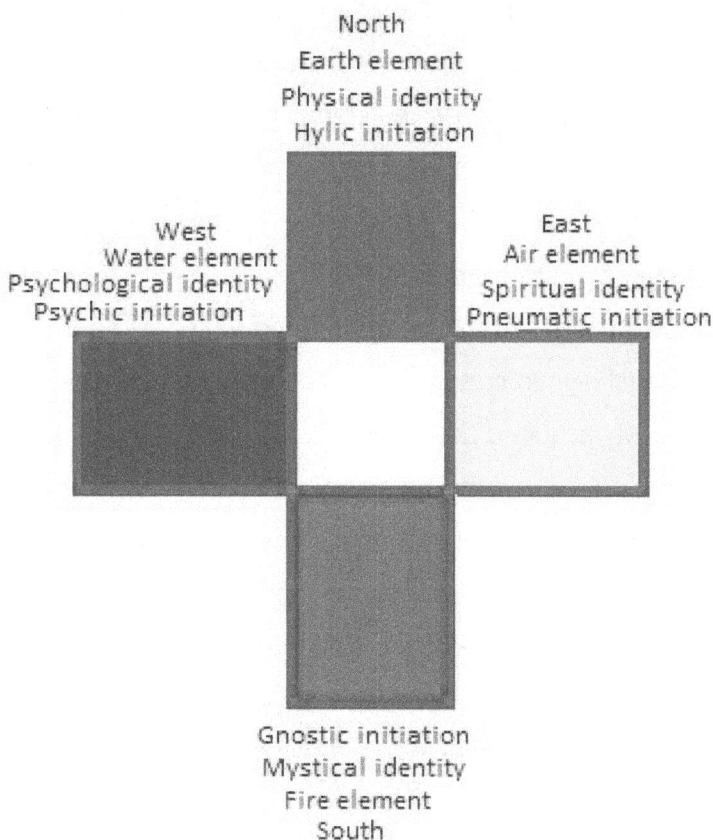

North
Earth element
Physical identity
Hylic initiation

West
Water element
Psychological identity
Psychic initiation

East
Air element
Spiritual identity
Pneumatic initiation

Gnostic initiation
Mystical identity
Fire element
South

Stepping further we arrive at the psychical understanding of life that it is connected to Water as element. To embrace this level one needs to detach the Self from earth and embrace the emotional experience of being an earthling. The 3rd level could only be realized if the understanding of feelings became a power that could build a bridge between the conscious and subconscious. It is the pneumatic plane where earthlings are able to connect to the substance of the universe and that is Air. Gnostic is the last possible plane. Here earthlings arrive to understand the Self as the part of the universe, and takes the personal responsibility for actions and thought forms connected to it. It can only be the element of Fire for it depicts the Light, the Knowledge and embraces the Whole through the connection to the Source. The 4 is also 3 + 1 however it will be a subject of the separate chapter in the book.

Throughout the 22 thousand odd years of the 5 Sun Ages, the equal legged cross has been used by many as a symbol for their newly acquired belief system. With the change in interpretation the original symbol faded into the background for it was dressed up with irrelevant objects and forms to fill in the gaps caused by the inadequate information about the Magnum Opus. These additions created new energies and thought forms that completely diminished the origin. However, the self-creative power of the Great Work cannot be suppressed. It is in every cell of the body and mind. It is in the subconscious, waiting to be discovered, understood and blended into the cycles of life.

Throughout our incomplete lives we have a feeling that something is missing and we arrive to understand that happiness cannot be achieved without it. It is the key to the subconscious, it is the key to the Haya Sophia, the Highest Knowledge, and it is the key to the universe. Therefore, Knowledge is the Key to the Source.

In this book I attempt to awaken your memory by building a bridge between the conscious and the subconscious. I talk about energies in a physical sense. I talk about ancient numerology with ancient astrology; everything that can be physically proven. I do not take on any wildings that cannot fit into my philosophy I call AKIA, for everything is interrelated therefore cosmic knowledge is a mirror of the unseen soul.

To help understand I give you the AKIA mantra I put together and encoded for my students:

AKIA INVOCATION

Great Creator, who created the universe, with me in it,
to look after and further your magnificent work,
that I accepted in good faith,
but could not always deliver,
because through my self-centredness
I chose not to see only look,
not to listen only hear,
not to feel only think.

13

Without understanding nature's harmonious cycle,
I stepped out of it, not suspecting,
that I would not be protected
and I would become an instrument of outside forces.

Please, give me the strength to forgive myself
for every bad deed I committed against
anybody and anything - including myself –
wisdom to others to forgive me.
Show me the way back to nature's cycle
where I can live in peace and dignity,
without indulging in suffering,
in a place, where love is unconditional.

After going through certain exercises, we say this mantra during the 5 days of the full moon period that goes from 2 days before, the day and 2 days after. The numbers are very important that is why we do it 13 times a day. The mantra evokes a channel with the help of the Moon energy and stimulates the memory. We say this mantra until one day we'll notice that the silvery thread of the Moon doesn't go away but keeps us connected to the Source. We arrive back to the cycle of nature and live happily ever after. Here I need to remind you that happiness is a state of mind and not a momentary joy.

1st Secret: The Soul and its Journey

1. Becoming An Earthling

When somebody gives birth, in Spain they say *dar a luz,* meaning *give to light.* By doing it one opens the possibility for an organic energy to grow. If this organic energy is guided and developed in the right way, it eventually becomes the source of light itself. It would reach the highest level of existence, the Sun man, the Ra that radiates and shines upon everything and everybody around, to ease the path. Therefore, when somebody gives birth, she actually *gives light.*

Every organic life form on Earth needs light. When you put a seed into a pot of soil you usually hide it in the dark so it becomes stronger in this dormant state. Then it will be eager to get out of the dark and search for the life force of light. However, if the seed stays hidden for longer than supposed to, depression sets in and it might give up on life forever. When the shoot appears, the seed arrives at the next stage of its life and becomes a plant. This example stands for all organic energies including human beings.

In the New Age we talk about the various aspects of light with ease. However, we rarely mean the above-mentioned Spanish verb. There are Light-workers, Light-eaters, Warriors of Light, Light-beings, Light-healers and I could go on and on and on.

Light-workers are earthlings who understand the energies of the universe. They are healers of the planet. The Warriors of Light are earthlings who fight for the Light. Light-eaters can digest light and do not need food. Light-beings are those, who incarnate onto Earth from time to time carrying important tasks. Light-healers heal with light. And Light givers invite souls down to Earth to fit into the ready-made costume generally called the physical body.

It is the place where everything begins, as far as we, human beings are concerned. The first descend to planet Earth. It is the moment when the soul becomes an earthling. It is the time when the light is born.

Souls from many planets are waiting for the opportunity to taste earthly living. Most of these planets, like Mars, Venus and Neptune, are in the same Solar System as Earth. Others like Leo, Aries, Gemini or Cancer are part of the 12 star formations zodiac that *ruled* people for about 5 thousand years. Although they are not in alignment with the planet any longer, therefore their effect on Earth is almost non-existent, souls living there still favour Earth as an exciting destination to camp out for a while. The 22 star formations *Lost Zodiac* also willingly *lends* souls to be part of the miracle of the Birth of Light.

Earth, by its ancient name Keta, is a very unique planet. It is like the essence of the universe; the only planet to carry the knowledge that has ever existed. To know Earth is to know the universe. Sometimes it makes me wonder, why earthlings want to observe other planets when they are still so far away from knowing their own. The *neighbour's garden is greener* seems to be a global effect.

Bearing all of this in mind Earth is like a school with only intensive courses that souls should enrol at least once in their infinite lifetime. The courses do not need entry exams and they all promise the opportunity of the necessary evolving as the sole purpose of all souls. When a soul decides to descend, it enrols in an *individual course* based upon its ability, strength, curiosity, courage and ambitions. After making a decision, the soul comes into the Higher Plane of Earth, the upper layer of the planet's aura called Shambala, to discuss the possibilities. Here the soul meets the first set of guides who help tackle the initial years on Earth. There would be also somebody representing the Alpha & Omega Council of the universe to give an additional task to fulfil, and to help choose the family to be born into.

Human beings like to think that they choose their children. Many of them pay substantial amount of money to control the gender and the time of birth. It is an illusion to think it possible. Parents only give their genetic appearance, physical structures and certain inclinations in behaviour patterns and inheritable diseases to offspring. They might be able to control the gender of the child with the help of medication, but it very often backfires. As a result, babies are born with confused genders, weak structures and often as disease carriers.

In this sense, a soul in waiting finds a physical body to *jump into.* The gender, the colour of the body, the social background, the family structure and all inheritable illnesses are considered by the incoming soul. This environment produces the soil for growing. The actual jump happens at half term, the moment the foetus moves for the first time. After that, for four and a half months the soul is virtually in the hands of its physical parents and its surroundings. It hears everything, it understands everything, and takes snips of the fragrances around, tastes incoming energies in the form of food, and throughout this time tries hard to maintain the situation. In the womb the soul becomes used to the physical body, observing its development, learning to use the senses and getting used to the emotions of the environment it chose to grow up in. The experiences of these 18 weeks would give a solid foundation for its earthly life. The balance of new experiences and protection should be established by this point in order to provide the child with curiosity and stamina while letting it gently know that help is always available. And there is a lot that souls need to get used to. Everything is sort of permanent on Earth. The permanence derives from the necessary usage of the physical body. The body structure itself carries a naturally unchangeable gender that would give a strong direction of living. Surely not many parents–to-be think about the influence a gender has on a child's direction. They usually say: *It is better to have a boy first* or *I am so happy it is a girl* or *I would have wanted a boy* or *It is another girl* and I could go on and on. Can you imagine how the child feels hearing these

18

remarks?!

Human beings have children because, according to them, it is the most fulfilling part of life. I emphasize the word *have*. This verb is the source of every misunderstanding, every emotional trauma and every upheaval in life. Ironically every subject in Earth School circles around this word.

One doesn't have a child. One gives light, an opportunity for a soul to develop and the possibility for the Self to learn during the process.

We need to establish that everything and everybody is energy and as such has light. Light, that comes from within and faithfully mirrors the current state of the being. The more developed the soul is, the more light it projects out and adds to the life force of the planet. Until one day it becomes the light itself. It reaches the state of the ultimate Light that has no Shadow.

The path from a light-bearer to an illuminated person, it is when the soul becomes light, is very bumpy indeed. The first challenge is to learn about the existence of such a path. Like every important thing in life, the path is hidden. Very few talk about it and even less grasp the real meaning. It is a personal Camino. It is an inner journey of self-discovery and development. This road doesn't lead to Santiago de Compostela or any other popular places of pilgrimage that are conveniently serving Christianity. It is a spiritual road, not a religious one. Religions, with their set of beliefs and practices don't give you the freedom to set foot on this path. All religions are codified in one way or another and centred upon moral claims about reality, while the only aim of spirituality is to reach the Source and unite with it. This is the sole task of every earthling.

Now that the Great Cycle of human existence ended, light becomes the centre of attention in every way yet again.

Although I am going to talk about cycles at large, I think I should mention something about the Great Cycle here. It is the 5 Sun Ages that began 22.250 years ago. The beginning of the first age would coincide with the descent to Atlantis. This cycle ended on the 28th of December 2012 Common Era. It is an astronomical event, or I could say astrological, for modern sciences divided ancient astrology into two separate bases of knowledge and announced astronomy as a science. This was an unfortunate deed, for everything is interrelated and one cannot be viewed without the other. By today we are well into the Golden Era, fighting with the darkness and desperately try to decide the direction we want to take on the evolutionary ladder after the Quantum Leap.

Light as the Fire element comes like Knowledge from above. It is part of the macrocosmic triangle that is getting ready to merge with the microcosmic one.

The Magma, the Fire, the light, the actual Knowledge in Earth's memory in the centre of the planet is making courageous and drastic movements to connect with the ever-lasting Light of the universe.

Here I remember the DVD I bought in Uskudar, the Asian side of Istanbul. It is all about the creation from the Muslim point of view. The title *How Allah Created Colours* made me very curious for it is widely understood that everything we see is an illusion for we do not actually see the object or subject but catch the broken light that mirrored back to us. The lighter the colour the more we can *see*. Our vision of things also depends on the physical structure of our eyes as individuals. However, the decisive element comes from the mind. When we look at something we only focus with one eye; sometimes with the right and other times with the left. The choice is made by the mind and it greatly depends on the understanding and the inclination of the individual. The right eye notices the physical appearance while the left looks beyond that. Although both send information to the conscious and the subconscious the final picture is drawn by the mind. We *see* what our mind allows us to see. For example, when a randomly-gathered group of people look at a simple table, some do not even notice its legs, while others notice its style, colour, height, width, but very few would see its energy flow, its energy centres, the worker's energy and the tree it originates from.

Let us get back to the DVD now. It is truly beautiful. The message is that nothing has a particular set of colours but the structure and the substance of the object we are looking at breaks the light in a certain way to send a particular message to the brain making us believe we see colour. This observation

21

carries great sense and coincides with my understanding of life. I mentioned it earlier that everything is interrelated that is why it is not only difficult but rather impossible to focus on these subjects separately. Whatever happens I promise to get back to the main stream.

From an earthling's point of view, we talk about souls and robots living on Earth. To follow the train of thoughts I elaborate on souls and leave the robots for a later stage.

A soul is a Knowledge, that is able to multiply by division.

Knowledge is the data of the particular energy. The word energy derives from the Greek *Energeia* meaning *action, movement*. It is one of those words was mistreated by globalization that transferred its essence to less important meaning. Energy is life itself. Everything that is alive moves. Energy never disappears, it only transforms into different values influenced by surrounding energies. I do realize that we usually talk about energy as a mass. However, every mass centres upon a core that actually gives that particular mass individuality. It is the main data of the mass, the strongest point that carries the characteristics of the whole. According to the data all energy mass has speed, frequency, colour, sound, taste, substance and smell. It also has a polarity that is either positive or negative. Naturally it doesn't mean good or bad in any way; it is only the reigning polarity of the energy.

In the ever-expanding universe everything is energy; either organic or non-organic. One might say dead or alive. The difference between the two is that the organic energy goes through rapid changes, sometimes even self-healing while the alteration in the latter is far slower and more permanent. Planet Earth is an organic energy as is everything that springs out of it. Regardless of the state, both carry data. Therefore, both represent certain knowledge they have acquired during their existence. For example, when I look at my table, I see a dark brown nicely-polished four-legged furniture with a comfortable height and width to cater for my needs at work. I also see an energy with three major energy centres that you might call chakras. Its energy mass that we could call aura, is light green to light bluish in colours with some hint of brown. When I look further, I see the tree in a forest near the Nordic Sea before it was cut out and used for furniture. I could tap into each level of the procedure and would be able to talk about the life of the workers, the company, the designer, the store and the transporter. This information, this data is the knowledge of my table and makes up its energy field. On the other hand, when I look at my next door neighbour Aida, on top of the usually-observed features I see an energy mass with seven major chakras showing her general physical and emotional state with the momentary situation added to it. The general state is made up of the past lives on Earth, karma and unfinished businesses while the momentary would tell me if she is in a good mood or not and the way she feels about the world at the given time. This knowledge about her would come to me mostly through sounds and colours with additional help from other senses.

With our limited understanding we see life as the cycle of the microcosm that is Earth, rather than being part of the greater cycle of the macrocosm that is the universe. The easiest way to demonstrate this interrelation would be on an equilateral triangle. The equilateral triangle is the 2-dimensional sides of a pyramid with an equilateral rectangular base.

According to the ancient Egyptians there was the very first dot one would call the Creator Force that projected itself out to become 2 dots next to each other. After endless projection the dots made up a line. It is a very good way of grabbing the essence of creation, particularly because we look at everything as 2 dimensional. I go a bit further and say that the first dot had to go through certain experiences and development to reach the highest level possible the crystallized Knowledge and became The Source, The Pyramid, with a perfect square as the base with 4 perfect triangles to make up the sides. It was the first knowledge to reach the ultimate level and was able to multiply by division. I plan to talk more about this subject later on in the book.

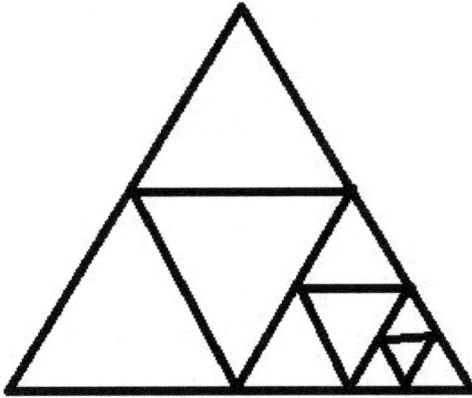

Pythagorean perfect triangles

Meditation to Meet Your Guides

Every earthling has 2 spirit guides at all time. Not more, not less. They are souls from a higher plane with excellent astral travelling capabilities. They travel between dimensions and time zones to give you the help you ask for. Guides understand Earth for they have lived here for many life times. The 2 spirit guides assigned to you are available for 24 hours a day to assist you with your questions or decision makings. Bear in mind that they do not interfere in your life unless it is really necessary but they are always ready to answer your calls.

They usually keep the last earthly appearance they had at the time they left the orbit of the planet in order to make you feel comfortable. Do not be surprised to see or sense an energy that belongs to a baby or a child when you are looking for your guides.

Some earthlings are caught in the religious web and they focus on seeing great prophets or a figure of religious importance like Jesus, Virgin Mary, one of the archangels and so on. Others are hooked onto the idea of having departed ancestors like grandparents or parents for their guides. Due to the religious entanglement many would call them guardian angels in the hope that whatever happens in life they would be taken care of and no danger could come to the soul. I would like to bring your attention to the difference between a guide and a guardian here, putting emphasis on the angel types. A guide is someone who is wiser than you are and able to answer your questions or help choose between possibilities. Guardians are protectors; they are there to prevent unwanted events and get you out of every trouble whatsoever regardless your deeds or words. Do you really think they exist? What is happening to whole nations falling victim to other's bullying nature? Where are their angels? The road to spiritual enlightenment is not easy to say the least. Your guides show you the path if you express the desire to find it. They would keep you on the path however they would allow you mistakes, sometimes even push you into situations for the sake of gaining the experience necessary to understand.

Knowledge comes from experience. It is the only way to learn. As you see it is not a choice but a necessity to meet your guides.

The practice

The best way to perform this meditation is during the 5 days period of the full moon. Wait for night to fall when the moon energy is the strongest.

Take 2 white candles and put them about 4 inches (10 cm) apart on a table next to the window. They might be of any size however tea candles in a metallic holder are not acceptable for they do not serve the purpose of the ritual. Burn an incense of any kind to cleanse the place and balance the energies. Light the candles. Keep a piece of paper and pen at hand. Extinguish every other form of light in the room.

Sit down comfortably, facing the window and the candlelight. Look at the flames. Imagine that they connect with the moon and form a channel. Through this channel you will receive answers to your questions. Think about your life how it is and what it is you want to achieve. Keep the connection with the flames. Think about your spirit guides and express your desire to meet them. Do not be afraid. Ask them to give you a sign on arrival. You might experience a tap on your shoulder or an itch on your ear. Whatever it is, remember it for they will use the same signal whenever they are about to communicate with you. Ask for their names. In this aspect listen to your intuition and write down whatever comes to your mind.

When you finished with the conversation say bye-bye and extinguish the candles. Use a candle extinguisher for blowing tends to carry away some of the fast energies that you actually need. You may reuse these candles.

Warning!

I have been teaching and using meditation as a tool for a long time and understand the danger might occur when doing certain meditations without proper guidance and protection. It is my priority to keep you safe at all-time however to fully achieve that you need to follow my directions word by word.

2. The Meeting of the 2 Triangles

After establishing the basic structure of the universe, I focus on the sides of the pyramid because understanding of the perfect triangle is essential to comprehend the link between the universe and human bodies. Talking about triangles let us start up with the 10 real numbers. I am aware of the modern views towards real numbers however, I find modern sciences to be distorted to say the least, therefore I am more comfortable relying upon the ancient knowledge.

We have established that everything is energy in the universe, and as such, carries data. This data arrives to us via our senses:

the fragrance comes through the nose, the taste through the mouth, the substance through the skin, the sound through the ears and the view through the eyes. If you want to sum up an energy we allocate a real number to it as the result of the particular data. Let us look at an example: a spicy smell with a deep sound, sweetish taste, rough touch and an olive-green colour would come into a number 4. However, this number represents the blend of the details. If you are interested in separate values a more detailed number could be assigned to the energy: like 62320, let's say. It is still 4 as a real number – $6+2+3+2+0=13=1+3=4$ – however the number allows you to see some details of the particular energy. As you can see the universe is made of numbers after all. The perfect triangle has the number 3 allocated to it.

Out of all the 10 real numbers - 0 to 9 - the 3 is the most important. Further important numbers are the 5 and the 7. The first depicts the connection to the universe; that is why the five-pointed star is the symbol of the hidden knowledge such as occult. The latter is the number of major cycles; amongst others the Moon and also serves as an evolutionary level.

There are two sets of three: one is down on Earth and one is above in the heavens. The three is the symbol of the whole, the perfect blend of the 2 poles and the essence of living. It is the knowledge, the Haya Sophia. It is the Great Work of the Source, the first soul that was capable of multiplying by division.

In pagan and shamanic movements, the 3 angles are the man,

the woman and the child. The child is the connection between the 2 poles. The 2 genders and the child are symbols here. In our minds they usually depict the nucleus of human existence, the family.

However, the actual meaning of the image carries a deeper understanding of human life. The male is representing the Earth energy, for males are usually more earthbound than females. They are more traditional, have more respect for the conscious and more boundaries. While the female represents the Water energy, being emotional, letting the subconscious out of the bottle and have mobile boundaries.

Then we come to the child. It represents the Air element, for it is innocent of earth-bound thought forms, traditions and layers of unnecessary education. It has the third eye open, capable of channelling, almost a clairvoyant, seeing and understanding the macro and the microcosm. It is connected to the Source and by the physical body the connection to Earth is secured. This is the energy that every earthling should become, and also the highest level every earthling can become. I do not mean that one should preserve the innocence of a child, but through experiences one should arrive at the conscious understanding of this energy. The 3 is also the number of compassion and love. Against all beliefs these qualities are states of mind and neutral in polarity.

Translated to our bodies we have the physical, spiritual and the astral body. I am aware of all the different interpretations around however one cannot ignore the structure of the universe and the interrelations of energies. Everything has to fit into the jigsaw puzzle of the Great Matrix.

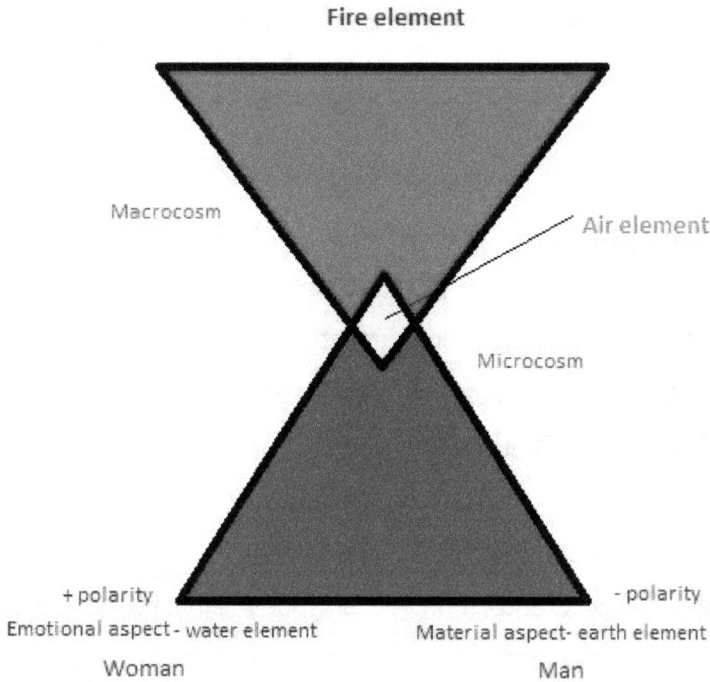

Fire element

Macrocosm

Air element

Microcosm

+ polarity

- polarity

Emotional aspect - water element

Material aspect - earth element

Woman

Man

Let us talk about the most obvious of the 3 the physical body. It is, as everything else, lent to us to use while we are here. We have it because it is actually necessary for our stay.

Almost everything we do on Earth is connected to the physical body. Without it there is no sense of being on Earth. It is an essential, and I would say, the only tool in Earth school. All our experiences come to us because of, and through the physical body. We work to gain money, to have a place to live, for the physical body is fragile and needs a shelter. We buy food to feed it, car to carry it, and every other deed really revolves around caring and satisfying the physical body.

But there is a *Catch 22* here. While catering for the body, the essential tool for the experience needed, we become more and more earthbound with workplace, with our house, with our mortgage with our family and so on. This way we forget about the meaning of life and the task we should pursue while we are here, and the way to keep the physical body healthier and alive. I could talk about the physical body forever really, but I should give time for the other 2, mostly because they are becoming more important, since we are already in the Golden Era as the 5th Sun Age has ended.

First, I need to mention the astral body here. Representing the top angle of the triangle it is the connection to the Creator Force. When I say Creator Force, I am not talking about a male or a female in human forms, carrying out all sorts of mundane tasks. I simply talk about the beginning. The first Knowledge that was able to multiply by division.

The astral body is free to move, an excellent astral traveller, easily changes dimensions and time zones and brings information from all over the universe to ease our lives and help us to further our spiritual path.

I would like to mention something here as an example. More and more people have allergies nowadays. Over the years of healing, I figured that people, who do not understand their astral body or the Self, would develop an allergy of some kind. It can be easily rectified by healing and changing thought forms.

The astral body is the channel to the macrocosm and our inner senses. The third body is the spiritual body. Many studies mistake it for the soul. However, I need to press that the soul is the combination of the 3 as they become one.

The trinity that makes up the side of the pyramid is in everything. The 2 opposite poles and the result of their evolution is the basic structure of the universe. Each of the 3 is made up of the same trinity and so on. These are the segments of the universe. In the case of human bodies from the shoulders down is the physical, the head is the astral and the neck is the spiritual. They make up the Earth, Water and Air elements.

Let us get back to the segments. Each of them carries every characteristic of the whole energy mass they form part of. As well as this, they have polarity. This polarity is either negative or positive. It means that every little segment has more of either polarity. I need to tell you again, that it has nothing to do with the so often used "being positive" or "doing negative" at all. It really means that particular cells are related more to Earth or Water. These are the 2 elements we have to get in alignment with, to be able to pursue our spiritual path and blend with Air.

Every aspect of our life is a decision making. It is either conscious or subconscious however the effect is very similar. When you favour one road more than another, you touch the state of equilibrium for a certain period of time. One could say that you are at peace. The decision is followed by movements like deeds or thought forms that actually ruin the equilibrium you achieved by putting your votes down.

There are many of us who do not like making decisions for the simple reason that we fear the outcome; in one sense we are being afraid of the unknown.

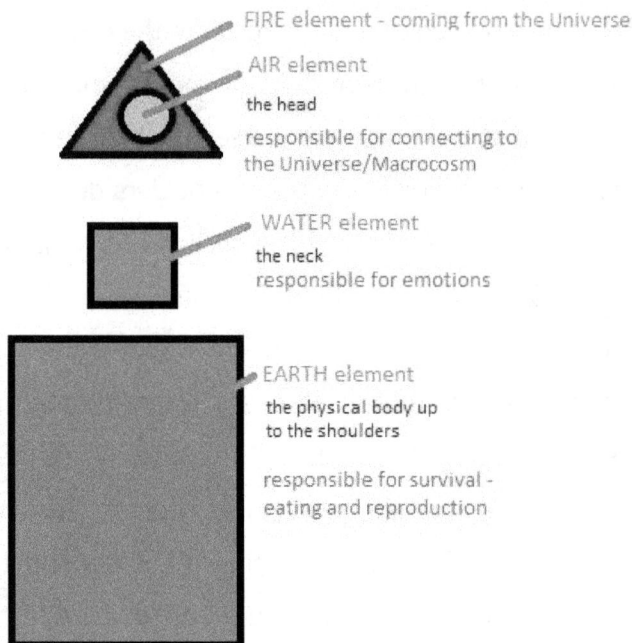

FIRE element - coming from the Universe

AIR element
the head
responsible for connecting to the Universe/Macrocosm

WATER element
the neck
responsible for emotions

EARTH element
the physical body up to the shoulders

responsible for survival - eating and reproduction

Bear in mind that fear is an illusion for you do not know the outcome. Understand that you cannot make bad decisions, for you choose the path that you are capable of taking at all times. That is your 100%. On the other hand, experience is needed for evolution and learning. Looking at it in practice, when you decide upon your next move, you connect your conscious and subconscious, meaning that you invite the Earth and Water energies to argue your case. The first stores the information you collected throughout your current earthly life, and the latter carries all the knowledge you gained during your previous lives. In the macrocosmic triangle Sun and the Moon create the 2 poles. They are not only essential for earthly existence but also the most influential channels between the 2 planes. The digestive system of an earthling is not equipped to take in the cosmic energies – although many people claim to be able to – until there is some interference from the Sun or the Moon. The third point of the triangle is the Fire element itself. It represents the cosmic knowledge gained from the interrelation of the 2.

Now that the 2 triangles are in the process of merging, the macrocosmic influence is opening our microcosm and putting a lot of strain on the earthbound humanity. There are 4 points in the yearly cycle when their influence is the strongest. These are the 2 equinoxes and the 2 solstices.

Naturally these events fall on the full moon day of December, March, Jun and September respectively. These are times when the macrocosmic man, the Sun, and the macrocosmic woman, the Moon, meet and introduce us to their magical co-existence. It is the pulling-pushing motion, the never-ending movement of the universe. The equinoxes and solstices are our time to learn, the time to get one step further and to leap into the brightness of existence. It is the cosmic embrace to assure us that we are not alone and we shouldn't feel lonely.

Here is the time and place to talk about the different types of human beings living amongst us. The difference is visible in their energy field. I say they wear different "uniforms".

There are the souls I have mentioned who come from all over the universe to take up an experience here. They belong to 3 groups: incarnated, reincarnated and *stayed behind*. First, I will talk about the reincarnated souls for they are getting out of fashion quite rapidly. With that, the *stayed behind* souls are slowly disappearing also.

Souls living in earthly uniform of the physical body go through certain experiences according to their choice and ability. From the spiritual point of view there are no bad or good experiences, for different events further the spiritual development of the soul. I might add that there is no good or bad at all for this expression is limited to individual understanding and emotional welfare. There are certain global beliefs about good or bad pushed into our brain and consciousness by the media and religions. However, it doesn't make them true. We are constantly working on our moral development to reach a state when we become responsible for not only our own deeds, thoughts and words but for that of others, following the understanding that everything is interrelated and we are part of the Whole.

I believe it is appropriate to give you the 13 points of the *AKIA-path-finder* here to aid my writing.

1. Time is an illusion that imprisons those without courage

2. Life is a constant cycle of searching for personal truth

3. Live without bringing shame on yourself

4. You must remake yourself in the eternity of your body

5. The night is not the end of a bad day but the beginning of a better one

6. The outside knowledge is the key to the wisdom within

7. Wisdom is the knowledge you can make use of

8. Material wealth you can inherit. However, true dignity needs to be earned

9. Everything you can touch is lent to you for this life. When you leave, you cannot take anything with you

10. Only through the universe you can reach yourself

11. The light embraces you unconditionally and disappears within if you let it

12. Imagination is the memory of the soul

13. The true knowledge is untouchable and changing

Although there is a fine line between good and bad, some deeds leave slow energies and some produce fast ones according to the emotional outcome. The first hinders while the latter boosts your spiritual education. Slow energies manifest in sorrow, unhappiness, depression, fear and anger while the fast ones lift your spirit to a state of joy, self-confidence, fulfilment, power and strength. Looking at the energies from the physical point of view it is quite natural that the latter would ensure speedy development and more joyous life. When these events become the past, they present you with a well of strength that you can fall back on and build your present and the future using the confidence gained. That is what some people call *good karma.* On the other hand, slow energies lessen your speed, sometimes to a point when you are stuck in the past, never touching the present and have no prospect of the future. That is what one calls *bad karma.*

I think it is the right place to talk about this karma business. Karma is a Sanskrit word meaning the consequences of actions. It is pre-religious so it doesn't say that somebody is constantly watching you and punishes you for your deeds but outlines the laws of attraction, the interrelation of energies. I would also like to mention again that happiness is a state of mind, a view of life and not a momentary joy. It is the understanding of existence. A happy person could still be angry, sad, even depressed from time to time but he is conscious about it.

In the universe everything has 2 poles as well: where there is light there is dark, where there is cold there is warm and so on. These mirror effects co-exist because one can only understand joy if endures sadness and vice versa. Since the aim is knowledge, experience is a must for it is the gate to wisdom. It means that what we learnt in the past should blend into the present so we no longer need to hang onto events. Well, we do not need to hang onto past events at all. When it happens, it becomes karma. It works as a shadow that follows and darkens the present. It also alters the view of the soul and changes reality. It is something we need to learn to deal with. I would say put a closure on it. The keyword here is forgiveness. You need to forgive everybody involved and you need to forgive yourself. Remember that one does 100% of one's ability at every given moment. Go through situations, analyse them and learn by adding them to your experience. Do not moan, blame or feel sorry for yourself.

The karma accompanies the soul until the closure is performed. It usually happens with the aid of a professional who is able to look into the past, finds the roots and helps solve the problem. When the karma is not cleared during the earthly lifetime, it rolls over into the next one. It happens when the soul departs from earth. When the time comes the knowledge that I call the soul, leaves the physical body behind and shoots for the planet of its origin. Fast energies are lighter so they are able to get detached from the core of the planet and have a safe journey home. While slow energies are heavier by nature and they do not have the required speed to leave the dense energy field of the planet altogether so they stop in the Shambala. From here there is only one way to go and it is downwards to start a new life and solve the karma that caused the soul's downfall. Egyptian wisdom is the most intact on Earth and it talks about weighing the heart of the departing soul and comparing it to the weight of a feather. If the heart is lighter than the feather it could take the journey to the sky but if it is heavier it would need to go down to the underworld. Later modern Christianity adopted this thought in the form of redemption when forgiveness is pressed upon the soul with the future concept of heaven and hell. These symbols tell you that if you do not take care of your life you may end up coming back with many unsolved situations and emotional trauma that will darken your new life on Earth.

Reincarnated souls go through the same procedure as incarnated, however the karma would be added to the life task. Also, their choices of families are limited for they need to be born back into the family that allows them to meet the soul or souls the karma is associated with. A mother whose karma is connected to the son might reincarnate into his family as a daughter in order to solve the problem. Unlike earthlings, souls are not attached to earthlings, not even those in the same Earth family. They follow the path towards evolution. It means that when souls leave Earth, they are no longer paying attention to the life of the other souls they shared a family with.

I would like to say few words about the *stayed behind* souls. These are what we actually refer to as ghosts. I differentiate between spirits and ghosts, for their energy and colouring are different. Ghosts are the souls that were too heavy to make it to the Shambala so they stayed behind with the intent of solving the karma. These souls are strongly connected to earthly living usually through one particular person who they blame for their misery. They are never happy, for living in limbo between 2 planes is not very productive. To solve the karma, they need a physical body. However, it can only be gained through reincarnation. Some ghosts stay behind because they are tied to an earthling. It happens when a soul in a human form refuses to let the departing soul go. It usually happens in families or relationships. By announcing that *I cannot live without him/her* and hanging onto the memories of the person the departing soul is tied up and unable to follow its natural path. I know many persons who keep the ashes of their pets or even relatives in their own house, because they cannot part with them. I think it is very selfish to put the responsibility of your existence on someone else's shoulder, dead or alive. One should have a meaning of life and it should never depend on anybody else's. Anyhow, these souls need help to release them from the tie. In our practice we do quite a lot of *ghost-busting* when we help the stayed behind souls through the gateway and release them to the universe.

Reincarnation was stopped when the great star gateway was opened on the 28th of February 1972. Since then, souls are cleansed to enable them to leave the magnetic field of Earth. Therefore, karma is slowly fading into the past. It was an inevitable step for the planet itself is in need of healing and cleansing. A large quantity of karma has been dumped into the planet by humanity over the 22 thousand odd years and Earth cannot take any more slow energies. This date marks the beginning of the mass incarnation of new souls to the planet. These are souls without karma, souls that have never lived here

41

before. It is the time when we started to talk about indigo children for the fast energy of their aura shines in an indigo-like colour. I'd like to state that every soul here is able to achieve that colour for the aura follows the changes in spiritual development and is never permanent. That is why we should look at the colours of the chakras and the aura brought to us from the Far-Eastern religions and philosophies as symbolic rather than educational. These colours are the blend of the 7 natural colours and that of the rainbow and they show us the interrelation of energies in the universe.

Now we have arrived at the delicate subject of robots living among us. Initially they look like the guy or girl next door. However, for trained eyes the difference is very obvious indeed. All the previously-mentioned life forms have 3 bodies on earth – apart from ghosts whom for obvious reasons have only one. However, robots have 2. They are physical bodies without souls. This is due to the over production of physical bodies.

Nature doesn't produce anything useless; nothing happens in vain. Each of the bodies has a particular task to perform. The astral body maintains the connection with the universe; it is an excellent astral traveller that leaps through dimensions and time zones to bring useful information from past, present and future. The channelling work we do and our communication with the guides arrive with the assistance of the astral body in the forms of dreams, intuition or fantasy. It is the master of the subconscious where knowledge and experience are stored.

Some schools call it the Higher Self. However, I find this expression unfit for the astral body because it is neither higher nor lower but the essential part of existence. While the physical body is connected to the microcosm and the astral to the macrocosm, there is a body to keep the connection between the 2 and that is the spiritual body. These 3 together are the soul. Their teamwork leads us to fulfilment, to spiritual growth and to the wholeness we so desire; however, as the manager you have to take care of your team. You need to give them equal opportunities to perform meaning that not neglecting or favouring one over the other. When you stop monitoring the work of a team member you sign the licence for neglect, disruptive work and laziness. When the team falls apart, the strongest member takes the lead. Since the spiritual body is a go-between, it has to come down to the physical or the astral body. In any case giving up the leadership causes the earthling to get out of alignment. As the result of the weak management the physical body usually takes the lead due to consumerism and the worship of the newly emerging god - The Money. In desperate attempt to reach the desired happiness, the soul starts catering solely for the physical body not realizing that the more they give the more it wants from them, until one day the soul is hooked and lose its strength to alter the situation. The condition with the astral body is a bit different. It cannot really take over as the physical body does, for its strength originates from the latter. However, it might receive more freedom when the physical body gives up. To translate it for everyday living sometimes earthly existence gets a bit too much with the everyday struggle of paying the bills, going to work and having no time for enjoyment. It can be a changing point in one's life and there is a possibility to turn away from earthly riches and start paying attention to the spiritual development of the soul. There is also a danger of going too far, missing the point of balance in this situation and ending up worshiping yet another god. It is usually the time when the soul joins a sect or a strong religious movement and gives up on the spiritual path altogether. Needless to say, that none of these movements are tangible for the soul who wishes to do the work it set out to accomplish. There are no 2 separate lives here as we tend to see just one which embraces the balance of using macrocosmic knowledge to ease and enhance earthly living.

I have already mentioned that everything in the universe is made up of segments. Because everything is interrelated, these segments are of the same structure; carry the Knowledge and have 2 poles of opposite polarities. When in perfect harmony it looks something like this on the top:

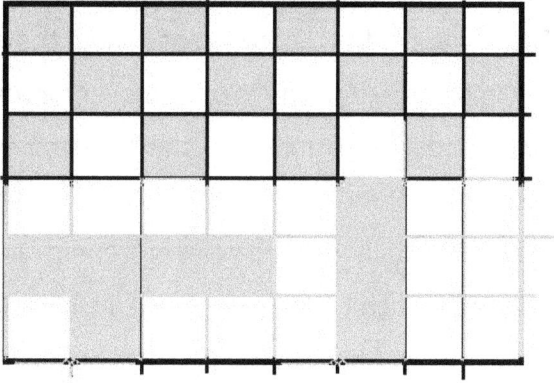

Then again, nothing that moves is ever in a perfect harmony. When a segment passes through its centre of gravity it touches upon this harmony. However, the fight between the 2 poles, the pulling and pushing power of the opposites maintains the endless motion of changes.

Although the 3 bodies, as separate segments, have their own centre of gravity they also have one together for they work as a greater segment. Information between segments is carried by energy lines. Where energy lines meet, a vortex an energy-centre is formed. It is actually an energy spiral going deep into the body transporting energies from the outside world. Depending on the number of lines meeting we are talking about minuscule to major energy-centres that we usually refer to by the Sanskrit word *chakra*.

Since the 3 bodies mirror each other, for obvious reasons, I have selected the physical body to demonstrate the work of the chakras.

The physical body has 7 major chakras, where 21 energy lines cross. I am aware of the different ideas about the number of the major chakras, but I urge you to think it over for the interrelation of energies and the structure of the universe would set the number straight. There are also 21 chakras where 14 lines are crossing and 63 with a meeting point of 7 energy lines. The latter is used by acupuncture to release the residue in the energy centre. In my way of healing the 7 major chakras would become important.

However, before merging with the 7 chakras I need to touch upon the New Age.

In the mind of many, New Age is a fashion movement. However, nothing happens in vain. We like to think that we control fashion. This is not true. When I was a fashion designer 16 years ago, I designed a collection far beyond my time for I was very open to the energy shift. Others play it safe and follow the global consciousness which is always many years behind. One way or another we are controlled by the new energy of Uranus that fully took over from the reigning Neptune and Pisces on the 23rd of February 2003. The shift in the energies is due to the precession of the equinoxes that I am going to talk about at a later stage. This is a fast and high frequency energy with a lot of promise in evolution. This is what people call the Age of Aquarius. However, the 12 star formations zodiac is not in alignment with the planet any longer so their effect is non-existent. Therefore, we cannot talk about the Age of Aquarius but the Age of Uranus. Let it be for now; I only wanted to show you how the major energy changes landed upon us.

Since the given date the physical body started its mutating process that brought changes not only into our spiritual but also physical wellbeing. We freshly after the end of the greatest cycle of humanity when the 2 triangles slide into each other and the macrocosmic fire element is pulling us towards the Source. As a result of this motion the chakras are drastically ascending bringing physical changes, introducing new illnesses and showing the incompetence of modern medicine.

The 7 Major Chakras and Their Tasks as they are now:

1. *Base or root chakra* is situated behind the caudal vertebra at the base of the spine. It holds the spine, takes care of the kidneys; all the feelings related to permanence would settle down here.

<u>Brief analysis</u>

This is the only chakra that stays where it has always been, to hold the spine and keep us connected to Earth. In the ever-changing existence this permanence puts a lot of strain on the energy centre that is visible even to untrained eyes. More and more children are born with bad body structures and bent spines. When I look at youngsters walking on the street my heart weeps; a great majority of them have no idea how to carry themselves and nobody seems to care. We take basic body functions, like walking, for granted thinking that it comes naturally. However, only the *what to do* is natural not the *how to do* it. It is due to the fashion with which we bring up our children nowadays or should I say do not bring up our children nowadays. It is a fashionable movement that children should bring up themselves to allow them develop the way they feel fit rather than take guidance. As I mentioned before, nothing happens in vain. Children are new souls with fast high-frequency energies. Most of them are volunteers and came down here to take part in this extraordinarily exciting time of changes we are very lucky to experience. Since they do not carry karma, their knowledge is intact and near the surface. They bear good connection to the macrocosm however they do not understand earthly living whatsoever. The guidance they are looking for doesn't arrive, therefore frustration and insecurity set in and the struggle to find a balance pushes them towards arrogance, despair, insecurity, carelessness and on many occasions depression. These are all starting points for drugs, alcohol abuse and suicidal behaviour. On the other hand, parents are new souls also and the guidance they received from their parents are not fit for the new souls for it embraces old moral systems, inbuilt fear and false pride. Apart from having a bent or a curved spine in many cases they develop kidney problems. As the organ responsible for ties and connections to material and fellow human beings, kidneys go through a lot, for the growing insecurity brings a tighter grip on belongings. I'd like to remind you here that security is an illusion and to pursue it is a waste of time and effort.

2. *Sex chakra* is in the navel now. It looks after the reproductive organs and sex related feelings.

Brief analysis

Due to strong religious influences and confusion about sexuality this is the most delicate chakra and the hardest to analyse. It is the true mirror of the human being. It tells you everything that is related to the earthling: its physical, mental and emotional state, its past, present and future, its behaviour pattern and beliefs. I do my best to unfold this energy centre for you without being very forward.

The first thought form we need to get familiar with is that sexual energy is the highest frequency energy a human being has access to. It is the elixir of life and the cradle of light. The next important thought is that sex is not the intercourse but it is in everything. It is the ultimate openness, total surrender and deepest experience. One can only be happy and open for development if one's relationship with sexuality is right. Nowadays it is very hard to establish an unconditional connection to sex. To look at it as the spring of light and not the greatest sin is a huge turning point that is hardened by a lack of proper education. When I mention sexual education, I am not thinking of the function of the reproductive system. I am talking about the way to discover the ecstatic beauty in nature and life. However, in everyday life the lack of understanding the essence of the art creates a base for many kinds of distorted relationships. Sons prefer their mothers and daughters get on better with their fathers. Mothers tend to look after their sons and keep them at home long after becoming an adult. When the daughter stays at home, she is the one who looks after the mother. Girls use their fathers as role models either way when it comes to choosing someone for partnership, and boys would look for somebody resembling their mother in behaviour pattern. On the other hand, when a son is born the mother forms attachment with the new male in the house and slowly detaches herself from the partner who is usually the father of the child. She would seek the affection of the son, would live according to his requirements and follow his opinion. The father would usually turn away from the mother and put the daughter on a pedestal. I need not say how much sorrow, pain and unhappiness comes from this behaviour pattern. It slowly eats you up and makes you forget about the real task in life, - your happiness and your individual aims.

There are certain misunderstandings we need to clear up. Although we use the expression, *we are planning a family* or *do you have a family* when referring to children, the word means a certain unit of individuals who help each other to maintain their existence and to reach fulfilment. One should never hope for happiness through somebody else, and putting this responsibility on children is selfish, for with this attachment one halts the course of one's own life and put a great strain on the children. At a later stage when you recognize your losses it is too late to alter the situation. Then again nothing is ever too late. You cannot change the past. However, with the experience gained you could plan a much better future for yourself.

This is the energy centre where detachment is formed and one learns the essence of the unconditional love we are willing to talk about even though understanding doesn't accompany these words. Without grasping the fact that peace, happiness and fulfilment can only be established within, and for that you are the sole responsible, life would never bring what you desire.

3. *Solar plexus* is 2 palm widths above the navel. It is to keep the body in balance and to look after the stomach, the gall bladder, the liver, pancreas and the nervous system. Feelings related to humanity at large settle here.

Brief analysis

The digestive system is the most complex chemical plant that has ever been created. It is set to digest all kinds of organic energies. However non-organic food would make permanent residues in the large intestines and alter the work of the factory. It is getting harder to keep the system working properly for we use a lot of artificial ingredients in our food, especially in the most popular fast-food products, the beloved Coca Cola and other soft drinks. Food as the largest conscious energy intake should be under scrutiny. There is a lot for responsible earthlings to consider especially if they want to stay in alignment with their own energy field.

However, it is not only food that uses the digestive system. All your thoughts about the world, politics, work, media, your private affaires and so on go through the machinery of digestion. This is all well however the problem starts when earthlings keep energies in the digestive system for longer than necessary and keep chewing on thoughts and events. The longer this happens, the greater the damage is, for this chemical plant doesn't make a difference between impulses and actual food, and the enzyme production keeps on. As a consequence, the body starts chewing on itself and in most cases, it results in physical discomfort and later disease. Language mirrors this view by stating that a particular human being is *eaten up by sorrow or worry*. In this case the feelings are displayed for everybody to see and generously added to the basket of energies we share. I call this the martyr syndrome for a painful sacrifice is made in order to alter the life of others. It might be a very popular behaviour pattern nowadays but its true meaning is very far from the fashionable idea we nurture. There are others who keep things private instead of exhibiting their pain. This conduct will build a safety belt around the waist and belly. The advantage of this behaviour is that the slow energy is not there to share. That is probably why overweight people are happier.

It is naive to believe that one could be redeemed by someone else's suffering. One cannot learn from the experience of others for it would never become knowledge. Also important to understand that sacrifice is a choice of the being with the responsibility comes with it. Since it doesn't spread joy or happiness - only sorrow and guilt - the accountability is vast. There is always a selfish thought behind sacrifice. Either you are a victim of a painful existence or you actually inflict the pain on someone else, pushing your views into the limelight forcing people to follow your opinion. To make the whole impact worse it usually happens in the name of love and care. *And we still call love unconditional.*

I think I need to add an important thought here: it is impossible to live up to the expectations of others unless you are in a closed community where everything happens according to set rules and regulation. There is always going to be somebody who does not particularly like you or talks against you. Tolerance and forgiveness are good companions in these moments and bear in mind that earthlings perform 100% of their abilities at every given moment.

4. *Heart chakra* is a palm width above the solar plexus. It is responsible for the heart, the blood circulation and the vagus nerve. Strong and shocking feelings affect this chakra.

Brief analysis

Although the widely-recognized belief is that feelings come from the heart it really has very little to do with it.

The only feelings landing here come through the vagus nerve which is actually in the throat. Sudden and unexpected events affect it hence why we say *my heart is in my throat.*

Spiritually long term or permanent slow energy feelings take up residents in the heart, especially a loss of any kind. I'd like to mention here that I find it very sad and also funny that we never hang onto anything happy. It is due to the slow energies of the Pisces era that put a gap between the 2 triangles and doomed earthlings to unhappiness. Fortunately, this deed is self-inflicted from the microcosm; the universe has never given up on us.

5. *Throat chakra* is in the mouth. Its job is to take care of the bronchial and vocal system, the lungs and the alimentary canal. Problems related to willpower, responsibility, dreams and communication show at this chakra.

Brief analysis

Everything arriving at the throat chakra goes through the thyroid gland which acts as a go-between thought forms and the body, making up the neutral part of the trinity structure that is in everything. As a reminder trinity of the Universal structure has nothing to do with any form of religion, it is the 2 poles of the positive and negative polarity and the neutral connection. However religious movements adopted and altered this form to fit their own understanding of the universe and still use it as the base for their rules and regulations. Bear in mind also that positive and negative are not fit to substitute good or bad in any way whatsoever; they are the two poles present in every segment, the mirror effects that trigger the motion of existence. The thyroid gland acts as the interpreter between thought forms and the physical part of the body. As a go-between it strives to be impartial, truthfully translates impulses and thoughts into chemicals to become understandable for the body; on the other hand, chemical reactions from the body become impulses to make it comprehensible for the brain.

The work of the interpreter is very important indeed. It has to be fit and fully functional to deliver the work. However, this duty puts a lot of strain on the organ and in many cases the stress causes malfunctioning. It happens when a mass production of thoughts floods the thyroid in an unorganized manner seeking translation all at once. I am certain it sounds intriguing however thought forms are organic energies as I am going to talk about them a bit later on in the book.

Apart from thoughts, the throat chakra also takes in feelings connected to responsibilities, unfulfilled dreams and wishes, communication skills and willpower.

Without responsibilities life doesn't exist. Basically, one is responsible for every effect one puts on the universe which one constantly does. Although an unspoken responsibility, it is the most effective contribution towards the Whole that earthlings are part of.

Dreams and wishes play an important role in the wellbeing of the *Throat Chakra* for earthlings seem to have many but act on few. From childhood, ideas about life, dreams about certain professions and lifestyles accumulate in the throat and turn into residues once being neglected for a certain period of time. Earthlings grow up fed on the media from a tender age and their wishes and dreams about adulthood would come from the same source. These dreams are usually shattered when they get to the stage of action for reality is nothing like a fairy-tale. It is all very well to watch films and read stories with the understanding that they are subjective views of other earthlings. Even history is written by someone who wasn't an active partaker and looks at events from a personal point of view. However, in most cases this guidance is missing and dreams remain in the comfortable dwelling of the *Throat Chakra*. Since it is the bridge with a 2 ways road, it affects both the physical and the spiritual bodies, meaning the conscious and the subconscious, therefore this residue is a real poison.

With my students we practice making inventories or taking stocks twice a year. We usually do them around the solstices because they proved favourable energies for it. I give you the recipe here.

Stock Taking

Take 4 sheets of A4 size papers. On the first write everything you love about yourself – interior and exterior. On the second you write things you do not love in yourself – interior and exterior. It is very important to be honest. Your writing shouldn't mirror the opinion of your surroundings or the mass consciousness but your own feelings about yourself. Bear in mind that everybody is beautiful and ugly, good and bad and so on. These are subjective opinions brushing the surface rather than giving thorough accounts. You might arrive at the conclusion that you do not really have opinions of your flaws and merits. Well, then it is time to get to know yourself. How can you understand about the world if you do not know who you are? Look into the mirror and observe. Watch your deeds and thoughts. Be flexible with your writing! You can add and remove as you feel. Do it for about 4 weeks and then look at the result. You might have put down certain unchangeable dislikes, like you are short, tall, brown eyed, overweight, skinny and so on. Well, whatever you do, you cannot become taller or shorter. It is a genetic inheritance you have to live with. The colour of your hair or eyes can be altered easily. If they bother you so much get on with it and change them. However, the rest should be accepted and loved for they are the part of you. Eventually everything should disappear from the dislike page. To live with hatred of yourself is a very dangerous ground for happy existence.

The third paper should contain all your dreams since childhood, and on the fourth you note down the ones that became a reality - whether they were helped by the natural course of life or a result of your conscious work. Children are usually hooked on certain characters for their extraordinary abilities, fame, beauty or pretty uniforms. Becoming a prima-ballerina, actor, pop-star, superman, pilot, conductor and soldier are amongst their dreams for the future. You might think they are not important anymore for time has put a solution on these dreams. This is a laid-back approach for time doesn't heal, it only pushes thoughts and feelings into the background. It works like a wardrobe. You buy new pullovers and put them in the front to give yourself the pleasure of looking at them. As time passes you wash them and place them back in the front. Only when you suddenly have the idea of reorganizing your wardrobe you find that many nice jumpers are in the back and many are ready to be given away. As you go through your wardrobe you remember events attached to each one of them, which you need to sort out. By doing this you achieve closure on the past. The very same procedure applies to dreams. Going through them you are able to close certain chapters and change thought forms in your life.

Be aware that people always give what they are capable of, therefore you need to stop blaming others for the events in your life. Your parents didn't enrol you to ballet school or singing lessons because their way of looking at life and your future didn't allow it. As a grown up to become a prima-ballerina is not an option any longer. However, singing is still an open avenue for you to pursue. Take it up and make the most of your life.

6. *Forehead chakra* is at the hairline or where it used to be. It looks after the nervous system, the left eye, the lower brain, the nose and ears.

Brief analysis

This is the place where everything happens. It is the meeting point of the 3 bodies – the astral, the spiritual and the physical – where thoughts and experiences are exchanged. It is the bridge between the conscious and the subconscious. Furthermore, it is the place where the macrocosmic triangle touches the microcosmic one and if circumstances permit, they start slipping into each other. This action is controlled by the *trinity of the eyes.* The left eye is the Water, subconscious and positive; the right is the Earth, conscious and negative in polarity; and the third eye is the neutral one keeping the balance through the right Knowledge flowing in with help from Light as the conveyor of cosmic experiences. This is the result of a very complex information exchange brought in by the senses. As I mentioned earlier, we only focus with one eye at every given time according to the initial viewpoint we stored in the brain. Using the right eye, we would be looking for a so-called *realistic view* while the left gives us some room for improvement. However, regardless of which eye we use the information received would end up in two places at the same time: in the subconscious and in the conscious.

The third eye or the neutral eye is called by different names to fit the philosophy or religion: God's eye, the eye that sees everything or it is preceded by the name of a certain prophet. I like the idea of ancient Khem, the place we call Egypt and usually call it the eye of Horus, for it fits the trinity structure of the universe: Isis, Osiris and Horus. Also, the Eye of Horus, like everything else from the same place is designed according to the function of the pathway. Therefore, the eye has 6 doors. They are assigned to the senses where impulses and information come in. It mirrors the evolutionary state of the soul with the hindering and forwarding behaviour patterns and thought forms.

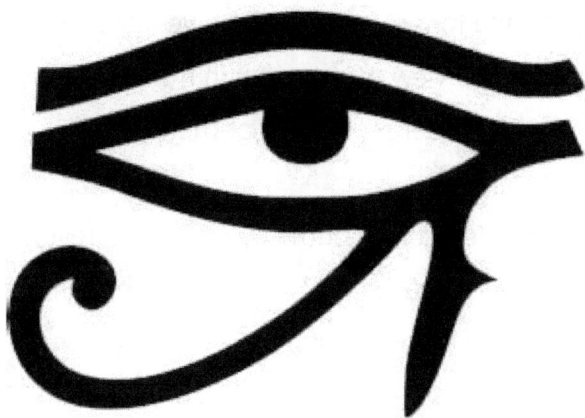

Remember that everything is energy for everything carries knowledge. The Eye of Horus mirrors the way we use our senses. The whole eye is 1 hequat by ancient Egyptian measurement that is depicted as a mouth for it is one bite: the biggest and the smallest segment. It is also the physical gate between the 2 cosms. While on Earth spiritual and physical nourishment arrives through it, on departure the soul leaves the body here. One hequat is 320 ro.

1. In the right lower corner of the eye there is a twig which we put into the ground to grow vegetables. It is a connection to the planet and is the gate of *touching*. Out of the 320 ro touching would take up 5 - that is $1/64^{th}$ of the whole.

2. The curved line going towards the left lower corner symbolizes the wheat when it is budding. The wheat is the food we put into our mouth. It is the *taste*. Taste is actually

touch and forms, meaning that we taste by touching different forms. This view puts tasting in front of touching and assigns 10 ro to the sense - 1/32nd of the whole.

3. The left corner of the eye is the nearest to the ear. It has the shape of a horn. Through this instrument the sound is tasted and touched. Therefore, *hearing* is the sum of touching and tasting. 20 ro are assigned to it - it is 1/16th of the whole.

4. We do not actually talk about thoughts as one of the senses, however they are very important. The long line above the eye represents the *thoughts* for we use our eyebrow to mirror our thoughts. They are considered to be the sum of touching, tasting and hearing. A thought is a silent voice. 40 ro are assigned to it; that is 1/8th of the whole.

5. The circle in the middle represents the actual eye. *Seeing* is the sum of tasting, touching, hearing and thinking. Receives 80 ro - to take up 1/4th of the whole. The horizon has no ends just like a spiral. Do not forget, the circle is a 2-dimensional spiral. As long as we see it as a circle there are limits to it. We create the limits.

6. The *smelling* is symbolized by the triangle nearest the nose. It is everything together. 160 ro are assigned to this sense - it takes up ½ of the whole.

Our senses have been distorted by ideas and belief systems. Fear prevents earthlings from using the gateways correctly. The notion *I believe it when I see it* puts a hold on spiritual education for seeing is an illusion as we only see the mirrored light and what we allow ourselves to take in.

7. *Crown chakra* is located about 10 cm above the head. It looks after the upper brain and the right eye.

Brief analysis

In this chakra there is the institution called the Mind. Information and impulses arriving through the forehead centre are sent here for further consideration. These are added to the already existing files or folders and then particular understandings and viewpoints are changed.

In everyday life Earthlings go through traumas, mishaps, joy, pleasure, hatred, envy, devilishness, fear, sadness, pain, love and other controversial emotions. Not many of us understand that all our deeds and feelings actually spring from the mind.

The Mind is a management centre, where a worker or workers - depending on the size of the company - process the data stored in the filing cabinet, called Brain. Some of the various folders are labelled as *Past Lives, Present, Future, Soul Siblings, Tasks,* while others are waiting to be organized. These are part of the subconscious, ready to be discovered and used as part of the knowledge, the wisdom that helps us with our endeavours on the path to becoming better human beings in the sense of unity and wholeness. Other ones, like *Dwelling, Work, Money, Car, Education, Holiday, Relationship etc.* are neatly filed in the very front of the cabinet for quick access.

The largest of them all, has *Miscellaneous* scribbled on the front with an indescribable hue of pink. It stores runaway files that sort of limber undecidedly between the conscience and the subconscious existing.

As an example, let us look at the first folder entitled Past Lives. It stores the data of one's ancestors, the soul-number, the basic abilities - so called codes - works the soul accomplished, events it passed through, experiences it had, battles it conquered or lost, and most importantly the knowledge the soul collected during its lives prior to the one it struggles with or enjoys here, down on this wonderful planet called Earth.

To be able to understand the purpose of these files, their interrelations and effects on every moment of living, we need to define certain things we keep talking about. The most important is to mention again that in the universe everything is energy in the physical sense. As such everything has speed, frequency, taste, smell, consistency, sound and colour. This is what we see in the aura. The mentioned characteristics vary according to the data and the knowledge they carry.

These energy masses are either organic, meaning living; or non-organic, meaning not alive. An organic energy is capable of reproduction, like earthlings, vegetation and animals, while non-organic ones don't have the tools to do so. The latter is the processed result of the former.

The sole purpose of an organic energy in the universe is to collect enough knowledge to multiply by division.

The impulses in the mind are all organic energies carrying data that has been altered by effects and counter-effects, helping or hindering the owner. If the management is good and the workers do a good job in the centre the results will tilt towards the helping end.

By observing and teaching the interrelation between the unseen soul and the cosmic knowledge, *AKIA* – the philosophy I have created - gives you the ability to discover and open the depth of the universe and the mind.

The *everything is interrelated* slogan offers ample space to the endless, the untouchable and unimaginable quantity of information, and in its explanations, an extremely dangerous way of thinking.

In this aspect the beginning, the end and the middle is vague for every end is a beginning of something and the middle of another happening. We can say the same thing about the other two. I put myself on the plate as an example and since this beginning was chosen by my mind it is not at all illegal to oppose to it. However, my choice sets boundaries on the train of my ideas, loosening or tightening their living space. The loosening and the tightening, as the choice of the beginning, depend on the momentary state of my mind, on my relation to the subject and the goal in front of my eyes. The information I have, my knowledge, my scruples, my upbringing, my schooling, my social background, my pledges and my conscience also play a decisive role in my deeds. They all alongside many more little ingredients send certain passwords to the brain to test and try the key into the locks of neatly filed folders and into those laying around in lazy untidiness. This action supports the strongest impulse, meaning the most urgent and most important task in the mind waiting to be solved. If I am lucky, one of the keys fits into a lock and I will find few refreshing and helpful thoughts behind the door.

Regardless of being conscious - formed under pressure, or subconscious - finds its way in without invitation - after creation the thought becomes an organic energy mass. Imagine it like a cartoon where the drawn figures' thoughts are being written in a little, balloon-like surface with an end pointing towards the person that masterminded the thought. This particular earthling would be the starting point of the thought-energy.

This is just an example of what is happening in the mind and as such, in the crown chakra. This energy centre is responsible for building channels to receive communication and healing energy from the macrocosm.

Talking about healing I'd like to give you a basic idea of the energy related procedure. As I mentioned earlier, like everything in the universe, the physical body is made up of segments. They are responsible for the constant motion within. Thought forms, impulses and effects gather segments of the same polarity to give support to ideas. When another task enters, they move to a different location. It is all well for the constant argument of the 2 poles keeps us going. The trouble starts when segments remain in the group permanently. It happens when the human being is unable to release an experience, a thought or a feeling and creates a still - therefore dead - patch within the body which develops into a physical unease, pain and eventually illness.

With healing we reorganize the segments and restart the motion.

Maintenance of the Physical Body

Exercising is still a good way of "keeping fit". However, not in the way we know. Chakras, as energy gates, need powerful muscles to open and close. When the chakra is blocked, the residue that is produced by the slow energy thought forms and the indigestible food consumed by the body, jams the gateway and causes the chakra to malfunction. Due to this event the unwanted slow energy residue builds up around the chakra in the form of fat. The rule of likes attract furthers the problem by taking only the slow energy from its surroundings.

Going to the gym unwillingly and jumping up and down is not the solution. You might lose weight but as you'll probably notice, it comes back very easily. The best chakra cleansing exercise is hope-chi. This is the name I created for the spiritual exercise I use during my workshops and seminars. Hope-chi is a string of slow movements working mainly with the joints and supported by meditation-like mental exercise on balancing and changing your attitude. I am not suggesting that you need to come to my seminars to do hope-chi. Your house is as good a place as any and by following my instructions you will be able to perform the exercise by yourself.

Sit down in a comfortable position. Straighten your back and keep your legs parallel. Close your eyes. Slow your breathing and bring it to a steady rhythm. If you have difficulty, try counting. Let us say count to three while inhaling and to three while exhaling.

While breathing steadily think about your problems one by one and imagine the very best outcome possible for each. Do not forget, that anything is possible. Limitation is a slow energy and as such, a problem. Solving a problem with another one is not the brightest way of getting ahead. With those bright images in your mind, start moving your hands and your arms, turning at the joints, the neck, the shoulders and the back. Stand up and continue with the hips, turning them round and round. Bend your knees and straighten them. Do this at least ten times. Turn your feet and toes. In the meantime, hold the bright image you created earlier. Keep on moving slowly as long as you feel comfortable doing it. When you have had enough, do not stop suddenly. Bring yourself back from the images, to the place where your body is, gradually and gently. Open your eyes. By this time your mood has changed, your thoughts are different and the world is a much nicer place to live in.

You might want to use coloured pictures or drawings to serve as meditation bases. Look at one that you feel the closest to at the particular moment you require meditation. Concentrate on the colours and let your mind disappear. Slow down your breathing and bring it to a steady rhythm as learnt in the previous exercise. Close your eyes and visualize the picture. Imagine that it is a gateway to a place where you find your answers by meeting the people you have unfinished business with. Here you have the opportunity to ask them questions. Listen to the answers. When you want to leave, say goodbye to everyone and walk through the picture gate. Then come back to the place where your body is. Feel the surroundings, the furniture, the light, and open your eyes.

It is always very rewarding to take long, early morning walks. It is especially so around trees. Trees are the lungs of the planet. A healthy tree filters 25 cubic meters of air every day. Most of nature's work is done during the night which is why the benefit for the physical body is greater in the morning.

With this thought we arrived to a delicate subject in body maintenance, sleeping. This is something we seemingly cannot get enough of. Sleeping is a defence mechanism. When the physical body gets tired of the abuse the human being puts it through, it sends out the warnings that it would prefer some peace and quiet for a change. If the human being listens to the warning, he may rectify the situation by getting rid of some of the slow energies the body is holding. If not, sleeping is almost inevitable, even necessary from time to time. The general sleeping time of the physical body is 6 to 8 hours a day but not more than that. After a longer sleeping period, the body needs time to recover and to switch over to being awake. I recommend 5 hours sleep during the night and a 15 minutes nap in the early afternoon. When you become good at meditation, you will find, that five minutes meditating can go very far.

Weight and the Physical Body

Being fat usually comes from some sort of unhappiness. Sometimes, when a chakra is "hurt" by being jammed, it gathers more slow energy to "cushion" itself up as a defence mechanism. The same method is used when the chakra is too open and unable to close when necessary. However, the key to this problem is love. You cannot lose weight healthily without truly loving yourself. As a thought form love produces fast energy which is important for combatting the slow ones causing the problem.

To arrive at this love, you need to look at yourself unconditionally. Look at your achievements rather than failures. Or better still, just love and appreciate. Be grateful. Find every opportunity possible to enjoy life rather than suffer it. After that the rest is easy. Joy produces fast energy and eats up more and more of the fat from your belly, around the waist and hips or wherever you have it.

Being overweight is not always a result of slow energies. Sometimes it is due to genetic inheritance. As far as I know modern medicine doesn't have a cure for genetic disorders. However, there are healers who can deal with genetic related discomfort or illness.

There are people who "suffer" from being skinny. If the body is physically healthy then do not worry about it too much. The same exercise applies to the overweight "sufferers".

Water and the Physical Body

Another excellent way of getting rid of residue and slow energy is water. It is the only substance that washes out residue and slow energy without producing any in the process. Apart from cleansing, water has another mission. Since a large portion of our body is made of water, it needs to refill. If your body cannot get the right amount of water from you, it will remove the fluids from the waste products of the body. Needless to say, waste products contain the slowest energy possible and they are very often poisonous. The lack of fluid in the waste products leads to a very common and painful disorder called constipation and the equally unpleasant varicose veins.

When the body dries out beyond quick repair, it becomes very difficult to drink water. You might feel nauseous and sick. This is because your body is used to the poisonous slow energy drawn from the waste products and it loses the capability to digest the fast energy you are introducing. In this case careful planning and patience is needed.

Water should be introduced slowly in growing dozes. Drink fizzy water if you must, but try to keep off soft drinks such as Coca Cola, Pepsi etc. They are addictive and full of residue, even if the label says: "no chemicals, no added sugar". Since everything in the universe is a mass of chemical compounds, I never understood how anything could not contain chemicals. So how do they make all those products if not out of chemicals?

I suggest you come to a stage when you are drinking 2 litres of water a day and you keep at it for at least 2 weeks. After that your body will be able to tell you how much water is needed to keep it reasonably clean. Plain, still, mineral or filtered water are the best for this exercise.

Now that we are getting ready to embrace the Uranus age, we need to exclude certain ingredients from our diet. On the top of this list are the three whites, the greatest enemies of a healthy or a *healthy to be* body. Those are: white flour, white sugar and animal milk. First of all, they are difficult, almost impossible for grown-ups to digest. Furthermore, the slow energy substance attracts other slow energies such as digestive waste products and blocks up the energy centres causing discomfort and illness.

Eating and the Physical Body

There are people on Earth who managed to reduce their food intake to almost nothing. However, eating is generally considered a necessity to existence.

Food is the easiest resource of energies. That's why we need to pay special attention to it. Buying your food is a very important part of the *healthy-to-be procedure*. You definitely don't want to buy your food in a store, supermarket or shop full of miserable people. Unhappy people mean bad management and because everything is energy, with the food, you take home a part of their misery. This is something one cannot afford to do.

The next step you need to watch out for the origin of the food or drink. When you live in a country knowingly or unknowingly you agree to it. You agree to its politics, its social standards, its treatment of people and its educational system. If you don't agree but still live there that is even worse. To fight against the general energy that surrounds you is a very serious action for your body. It is better to blend in or leave. This explains why people should eat the product of their own country first of all. And for better or for worse, we generally do just that but not always for the right reasons. Since we cannot live without explanations, we grab whatever is available.

The major astronomical movements I mentioned earlier are pushing the human beings to find their true home. It might not be, and very often is not, the country you were born in or the one where you are currently living. That is why some people purchase food from far away countries with a different weather and eating habits. If you belong to this category, I suggest, that you look at your life.

There are numerous food products available from more than one country. As the product carries the general energy of the land try to choose accordingly. Suffering, corruption, bad deeds, bullying home and foreign policies put their stamp on the imported products.

Vegetarian or Not?

It is becoming more and more fashionable to be a vegetarian. But is it good for us? Does it make any difference to our existence?

Vegetation is the most advanced form of life on Earth, holistically speaking. With their roots they feed on the slow but warm, healing energy of the soil while taking the much faster, white energy of the heavens. Unless poisoned or maltreated usually by human beings, the vegetation carries the most suitable nutrition for the body of the Homo sapiens to fit into the energy concept of the Solar System. So becoming a vegetarian is a very essential part of the physical and spiritual enlightenment of a New Age person. I'd like to emphasize "becoming" here. It is a gradual development rather than an immediate switch. There is no use force-feeding us with greens while dreaming about a juicy steak.

74

The body has to arrive at the stage mentally and physically where it can open up to the light without pain, free of misconceptions and vanity. There is another important thought: Do not become a vegetarian because you oppose mistreating and killing animals. A carrot is a being too, with excellent understanding of existence but because it doesn't speak, or rather you cannot hear its words, you do not mind killing it. Also, more and more people are having pets at home and pet food is full of animal substance. What about killing then?

In my healing practice I meet a lot of people who are having physical problems because they stopped eating meat without being physically ready for it. Sending them back to meat could do the trick, but it doesn't feel right. Instead, I teach them methods of cleansing that they are able to practice at home without me. This way the physical body gradually loses the residues and opens up the doorways necessary to welcome new eating habits.

4. Inclinations and Inheritances

I do not support the idea that we carry a code from our earthly ancestors. These codes are supposed to lead you to the trodden path of your grandparents, in some cases that of your great-great grandparents. They are also meant to transfer or continue the responsibility for their deeds onto your shoulders creating quite an upheaval and many obstacles in your life. When we look at the constantly moving universe, we realize that this idea is only wishful thinking by those who dislike change and dwell in the past. Or of those who want to implant fear and with that totally succumb to man-made controlling rules. It is a very dangerous idea indeed. The foundation is very fragile and totally dismisses the possibility of the Macrocosm by turning Earthlings into narrow minded robot-like creatures with very few choices about the future.

Earthly ancestors mean very little to a soul. Many people follow or re-live the life of a parent of the same gender believing that there is no choice; that this path has to be taken for it is karmic or simply fate. Well choices do not come to you by themselves. One needs to have adequate information to be presented with choices. Everybody has a choice but one needs to find those paths. For many people having choices is a curse. Different aspects need to be looked at and decisions need to be made. The other convincing feature of path- following is fear.

There are certain cases when one follows the footsteps of a parent without much thought and consideration and then when reality hits it is too late to stop the motion. Looking at parents as raw models can make or break the future of a child. There is far more to parenting than staying together and pretending to be a happy family.

There are also physical inclinations such as certain movements and ways of carrying oneself; likes and dislikes for food, drink, events and so on. As likes and dislikes are in the mind, I would not take it as a code. My parents divorced when I was 4 years old. I lived with my mother who was constantly blaming my father for everything and told nasty stories about him even though she was already remarried and had a new baby from the second marriage. One day, when I was eating sourcrout, which happened to be my very favourite dish, she mentioned that I was a lot like my father because I loved the dish and so did he. I put the spoon down straight away and did not look at a sour cabbage dish for a couple years until I had the opportunity to meet my father and understand him a bit better. I realized that he was not a bad person so it stopped bothering me that I was in any way like him.

Biological inclinations are very tricky indeed. Your physical body is the merge of the 2 bodies of your parents therefore there is a great possibility to develop inclinations towards certain illnesses or other behaviour carried by one of the merging bodies.

These tendencies are dormant until a key energy triggers them open. And here we arrive back to the interrelations of energies for it is the key to everything. Depending on the relationship between the conscious and the subconscious one carries a certain emotional state which works like a magnet and pulls in certain energies to interfere with the condition of the existing one. This is how these inclinations open and blend into the life of the unsuspecting victim.

As a healer I would say that these tendencies are not only

detectable but curable. Although this book is not focused on healing, I will make an exception here and tell you the way we work with inclination.

Everything important to an earthling is in the mind. Therefore, the mind enjoys special protection from intruders and slow energies. I grouped up brain functions and created 12 cells that are easy to handle and good to work with during healing. For extra protection I put those cells into the merkaba. It is spaceship for the soul we use during astral travelling and also serves as a protection for life functions. The door of the merkaba only opens for the owner. Every soul has a merkaba however one has to be ready in order to work with it.

On the dashboard of the spaceship there are the cells, all 12 of them in 2 rows as follows:

senses	recollection	movements	metabolism	thyroid gland	lymphatic system
grounding	emotions	reproduction	breathing	blood vessels	endocrine glands

The new souls have 6 additional cells:

root	consciousness	task	emotions	respect	responsibility

After the request is received and permission for entering is granted by the merkaba owner we take our place and start working. We find the root of the inclination; remove it, while the

78

patient is taken through the rehabilitating procedure.

Inclinations are changeable inheritances. There are also those we cannot change. I must admit I am only saying this because I have never tried to interfere with them. They are part of the contract the soul signed prior to landing here for this lifetime. Therefore, it is a part of their evolutionary journey and as such these inheritances are protected by laws of the universe.

5. Thought Forms – Energies around the House

By popping out of a brain the thought becomes alive. Like all other organic energy forms the thought need something to feed on. The pointed end turns around and searches for nourishment. This search is guided by the energy of the thought, meaning the words written on the balloon. The natural choice would be the person it was intended for. In the hope of reaching it in time, the thought starts its feverish search for the addressee.

It has been said that the thought doesn't count. And that the word or the deed is far more important.

The strength of both lies in the power of the thought.

Household Items

The so-called civilized home has a lot of gadgets that are perfect for bringing the energy frequency down. Now when we really need all the help to raise our vibration the surroundings have a key role in our well-being.

The most powerful killer machine is the internet. With the pictures and thought forms of consumerism, brain washing mass media, violence and corrupt behaviour patterns of earthlings it is definitely the biggest obstacle in our lives. The next most dangerous item in the household is the television set. With the zillions of channels coming from everywhere endless supply of slow energies take residence in the house. The third best is the mobile phone. When it comes with internet it topples all the others and becomes the number one enemy.

I have mentioned earlier that thoughts are organic energies and they are feeding on organic energies. Since similar energies like each other they would look for slow energy forms with low frequency. If they find it in the user then an exchange of energies take place however in the case of a user on higher frequency an adjustment needs to take place by implantation of slow thought forms. In any case there is definitely a loss in valuable good quality elixir. Today many people suffer from an anxiety disorder or depression; all of those are frequent users of the mentioned household items. If addiction sets in it has to be treated as any other form of strong bonding and slow withdrawal treatment is advised.

Other household items like a refrigerator, an iron, a washing machine and above all a microwave oven bring in a large quantity of slow energy through the electricity cable.

Feng Shui

It is fashionable today to copy Far-Eastern philosophies, healing methods and wisdom. Unfortunately, during the journey from there to other locations on the Northern hemisphere these methods go through certain changes. They become money making schemes wrapped in a very promising package. Feng Shui is one of the methods which created a multimillion dollars business and the only way it helps is through the belief system. We should not adopt it because it changes our way of living and thinking. Having mirrors and crystals in certain places of the house only works if everything carries the laws of the structure. In China they do not build a house or a road without consulting the energy lines and the laws of Feng Shui that actually deals with the interrelation of elements Water and Air.

I have few tips here for Western households:

When I talk about energy I do it in the sense of physics. Following this idea every energy has a certain colour. Therefore, it is logical that colours are energies. Out of all the colours gold has the highest frequency and is the speediest. It represents the Sun, knowledge, brightness, enlightenment and high spiritual awareness. It is the reason behind the high valuation of gold itself. As I mentioned earlier, numbers carry certain awareness and are important.

The stars I am talking about can be cut out of ordinary gold paper and placed where required.

3 pointed star

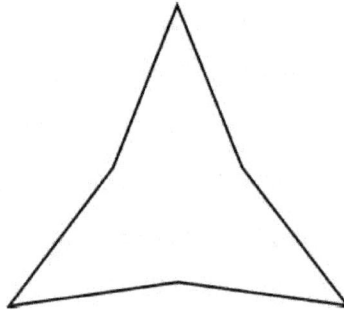

- It is against wind, fire and water when it is put on the front door, for it keeps out the surplus elements
- Above doors acts as protection
- It calms down hyper active children and animals
- It is advisable to meditate on it at least once a month
- If your place is damp, you can put it on the door
- Place it under the mattress to block infiltrating underground water stream

4 pointed star

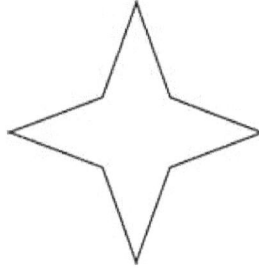

- It is the master eye opener and healer
- It is wonderful for healing the trees
- It is used to cleanse wooden things
- It seals secret documents when put on the bottom of the drawer
- It is also good for relaxation when meditated upon.

5 pointed star

- Is the symbol of the occult; the hidden knowledge of rituals and communication patterns. It also depicts Venus as the great knowledge-bearer and helper of earthlings.

83

- It can protect against slow energies and entities of the same sort if placed on doors and windows.
- Place it on the back of your laptop, PC, TV, telephone, mobile and all other electronic equipment to keep slow energy entities on a leash.

6 pointed star

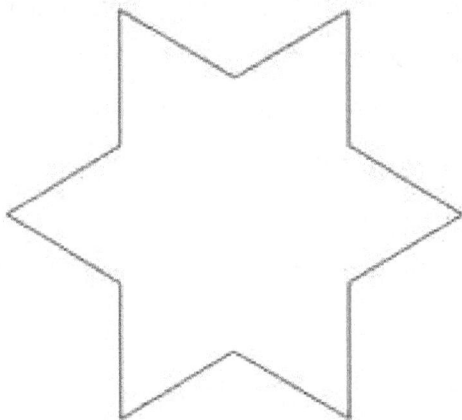

- It is good for balance
- It can be used to change thought forms and attitudes
- It closes gates between dimensions

7 pointed star

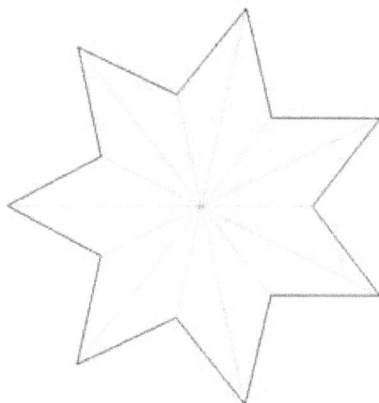

- It is excellent for chakra cleansing and balancing
- It raises the frequency of the energies
- It is used as protection against the willpower of others
- It is good for meditations with the Moon, Sun and the Stars
- It gives protection when placed on the Solar Plexus. Also helps in dealing with earthlings
- It is connected to Water element therefore it is very good for dealing with emotional stress.
- It is used against astral entities if or when you do not want them around
- It is excellent for keeping away the pulling power of Earth energies.

8 pointed star

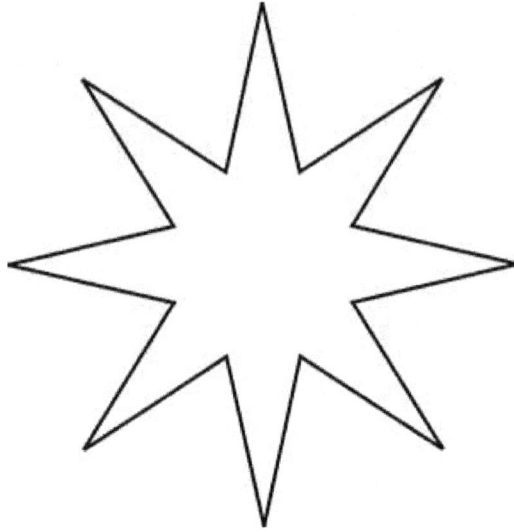

- It is good for people who are *floating* or *airy*.
- It is excellent to lower the energy frequency of a place and person.
- It is the best tool for keeping hyper children or persons in balance.
- It provides good overall protection for the energy centres.

9 pointed star

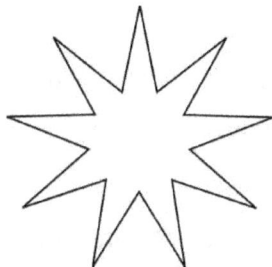

- It is the symbol of immortality
- It shows you the path towards unconditional love

10 pointed star

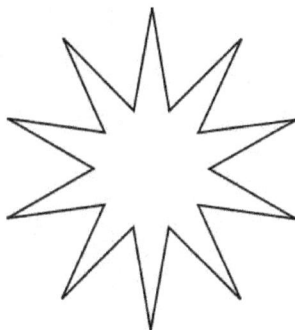

- It is the beginning and the end – the symbol of astral cycles
- It helps communicating with the guides and other souls from the macrocosm
- It helps survive certain unbearable situations
- It helps ease bad weather conditions

I am not exaggerating when I say that decision-making is the cause for most of our headaches nowadays. Emotional distress, nerve-related illnesses and digestive problems can all be a result of poor or non-decision making. I don't belittle the struggle and manoeuvre we put ourselves through in order to arrive at that very point, for having a choice is what we always want. Having a choice makes us comfortable and confident. With choices we feel safe. Nothing can go wrong with choices. The more we have the better it is. We feel in control and adequate; proud of our achievement. A lot of time is spent on building the outcome of these choices, one by one, until they fit into the microcosm of the owner. These pictures display success stories and we are in the centre, and we are certain, that life is going to be all right and we will live happily ever after.

Whatever stories you build in your mind, sooner or later the time arrives, when a decision needs to be made. And the pictures will start transformation procedure from achiever to loser. It happens because you actually have to act upon your thoughts. The choice you make could transform your future. Suddenly it becomes a responsibility. The beautiful stories of your success quickly change into doubts about your capabilities, knowledge and will power. You also begin to understand that the outcome is not entirely up to you, for there are hindering and forwarding elements you need to consider. Although both ends of the scale derive from you but it is subconscious rather than conscious. However, your whole Self is in it. Your intelligence, emotional and physical state, will – power, aims and desire and the eagerness to learn. As you are here to experience, by making choices the theory becomes deed and starts its journey towards knowledge. The degree of learning depends on your attitude to changes first of all. I want to remind you that by choosing you start walking on a new path even if you have experienced something similar before. The past doesn't exist any longer and we can never go back to the place or situation where we have been before.

There is also the element of shame. What if you do not succeed? How would people look at you? How would you look at you? Will you be able to stand up after a failed attempt?

Human beings want to believe that they are leaders; we are in charge of our lives. We always moan about freedom. Many people, especially in the spiritual and esoteric field think that they are free. "I am a free spirit!" one would say. But what does it mean? What does it really mean to be a free spirit? Just by involving yourself in esoteric or spiritual teachings you do not become a free spirit. It wouldn't even make you happier.

Because that's what it is all about. It is about the freedom to be happy. The freedom to enjoy life. The freedom to see the choices and take them without fears.

You need to understand that total freedom is only in the mind. People do not get it. We used to talk about the iron curtain and physical restrictions of people, but it is all on the surface. And you know that important things are not visible to the naked eye. Earlier it was established that fear is an illusion, because you do not actually know what you are afraid of. Here is my life motto, a Zen teaching:

God, grant me the Serenity
To Accept the things I cannot change.
Courage, to Change the things I can
And Wisdom always to see the Difference

It establishes the fact that wisdom is the key to everything. This kind of wisdom comes from experience and the great understanding of the universe. When proper selection is made, time, energy and emotion are not wasted in vain. Control and understanding are not necessities to happy living. Furthermore, neither control nor understanding exist.

In order to gain wisdom human beings need to be pushed to the edge at times to help create a purpose to fight for. By fighting people get stronger and gain experience. This way time is not wasted on decision - making but focused on aims.

In the interrelation of energies, we learn to change the fear, the suffering and the sadness into power and to direct this power towards a valuable aim.

Everything we do here on Earth is about the interrelation of energies in human relationships. These experiences further the understanding of the Self, the 4 elements within and around, and the journey towards the ultimate goal: the connection to the Creator force within. Without it the Fire element of the universe would go unnoticed and wasted. It is the condition to become the part of the whole and to find the balance we seemingly seek. As my experience shows this harmony or balance is widely misunderstood amongst earthlings. Out of the few goals we aim for this is the most common. We never stop dreaming about it however deeds usually stay in the background or begin an unrelated journey. We have been fed with fairy tales which show the struggle we need to go through to reach the "*and lived happily ever after*" state and it is always the consequence of marriage, if I put it loosely a couplehood, between 2 differently gendered healthy earthlings with some sort of wealth behind them to support the harmony they are after. This is a symbolic view of earthly living and should not be taken word for word. The "*what is important is hidden*" theory is in action here once again. The wedding of the 2 poles means that the interrelations are learnt, emotions understood and mastered and the 2 cosms are united in one. With the 4 elements existing in harmony the earthling is ready for the evolution and the quantum leap. This is the marriage we are after; in reality however, the meaning is concealed behind dogmas, spiritual and religious views that mirror the actual evolutionary level of their creator.

The "*live happily ever after*" concept depicts an imaginary state earthlings search for. "*I only want to be happy! Is it too much to ask for?*" we say while waiting for some kind of a miracle to provide us with the subject or object of our happiness. We do not realize that the question itself is the only obstacle preventing us from reaching a state of harmony. Primarily the sentence is pointed to the Self, and quite rightly I must admit, for happiness comes from within, whatever our understanding of the word is. Nevertheless, we mislead ourselves by pretending to be aware of this. However, on the picture behind this question there is always somebody taking up a very prominent place in the outcome. Why do we say that "*I want to be happy*" when it is conditioned on the presence of another person? There are 2 answers to this question: we either do not care or we do not understand. Neither of these conditions takes us closer to the goal due to the lack of a basic understanding of earthly living.

Earthlings are here to evolve through experience. Basically, there are 2 kinds of experiences: conscious and subconscious. Although they both further the journey, in this case I talk about the latter and not of money-making skills. Earthlings who are aware of the path set their goals with an understanding that they are only necessary for drawing the initial direction rather than an aim to reach. Random experiences are thrown in by the universe to help the evolutionary journey. As everything is interrelated these events are actually the consequences of the energy movements in your life. Earthlings who are spiritually aware would be grateful for and learn from both. Others would get angry, depressed, hurt and unhappy about the random experiences, and would hurry to reach the goal they consciously set without walking the path towards it.

It does not matter which way I look at the interrelation of energies in human relationships, the Self has to be built in order to understand that you are responsible for not only your deeds, words and thoughts but for those of every human being, because you are also affected by their deeds, words and thoughts.

It is very easy to get lost on the road to fulfilment. However, one thing is for sure: there is no easy way, and spiritual development is a must. The fear of being different keeps a lot of people away from this search and the misconception concerning the meaning of spirituality and religion only add to the task load.

Keep in mind that a religion is a set of beliefs and practices often centred upon specific supernatural and moral claims about reality. Becoming part of a religious group only requires acceptance of the mentioned beliefs; while spirituality is an individual and sometimes lonely path to walk in order to become one with the Creator Force.

Looking at our world at the moment there are different groups trying to push, sometimes even force earthlings into agreement of their theories of life by limiting their views of the universe and promising salvation for deeds they consider improper for a human being. Needless to say, the choice is yours. Occasionally one might be forced into joining certain assemblies but nevertheless the real and the only freedom dwells in the mind regardless of the behaviour pattern of the physical body.

Religious groups and individuals who denounce the exchange of energies between earthlings in any way, are hiding away from the pleasure, sorrow, happiness, sadness and other feelings encountered through this type of exchange. As practice shows, their aura is pale, the fire is missing from it together and their connection to Earth element is really strong. One might say that being connected to the Creator Force is all one needs, and that knowledge finds a way to flow into the consciousness of the individual. However, we are here to learn and go through certain events and to understand the Creator – meaning the first knowledge that was able to multiply by division – within. Without this wisdom one cannot get connected to it due to the dividend created between the 2 worlds.

Coming down to Earth is a choice. Therefore, turning away from earthly life is like hiding behind dogmas and excuses to spare the Self from hurt, disappointment and sorrow. On the other hand, it is an existence without the wonderful experiences of everyday events. Living in the physical body but putting on the shoulders of fellow earthlings to maintain it, is an unfair deed. Furthermore, these groups get what they want from others by using the most common black mailing system of shifting responsibilities and raising guilt in the uncertain and undecided minds. They might even say what they do is a sacrifice and that it is done for your benefit. Do not be fooled! It is a selfish act, to serve the ego by seemingly becoming egoless.

Talking about myself I cannot see why I should support somebody's earthly connection by feeding or paying for the necessities to keep it alive, when I need to look after my own and work for the support of those who want to live. I choose to take part in life, I bear responsibilities for my own deeds, I make choices and I evolve.

There is another very interesting group of earthlings: the consumerists. They only believe in what they see – which is obviously very limited – and they build their material wealth, indulge the physical body and go through their chosen experiences in life. This group of earthlings are connected to the Earth element. Occasionally, by letting emotions in, they hit Water and very seldom arrive at the level of Air. Fire definitely avoids this group. Do not get me wrong! We need money and having it is not a curse! But it shouldn't take up all your will power and purpose because you might just end up purposeless. Every human relationship is based on the evolutionary state of the Self. In the interrelation individuals should learn from each other through unconditional trust and love. This type of love is helpful and emotionless; the secret of which is to understand the fact that earthlings perform the 100% of their abilities at every given time. It is only expectation that belittles it. As the result

95

learning each other becomes the centre of togetherness. There are no right and wrong in viewpoints only difference. Observe and understand them.

2nd Secret: As above so below

1. The Five Sun Ages

As we slipped into year C.E. (Common Era) 2012 desperation and curiosity got the better of us, and we started to air new approaches to the recent astronomical changes. Although we freaked out, we couldn't hide from the truth. Step by step we arrived to the 28th of December 2012, when the 5th Sun Age ended.

I am sure that the date I put the end of the Sun Age on, caught your eyes. I am known for altering long-established dates mainly because they do not fit into the laws of the universe and I am also known for not failing with my predictions. The idea is that everything is interrelated therefore the basic structure of every kind of energy has to follow the same pattern: the equilateral triangle with the 2 poles and their meeting point. In the case of earthlings this triangle rests on the perfect square of the 4 elements creating a pyramid.

Important events can only happen when both poles are at their best and this is at the time of the Full Moon. I have mentioned earlier that against all beliefs equinoxes and solstices happen on the day of the Full Moon. Therefore, a Sun Age can only end on the day of the Full Moon, on the Winter Solstice when the new era arrives. This date was on the C.E. 28th of December, 2012. I understand the Mayan calendar very well and the conclusive date of the 21st of December derives from the false assumption of the time set for the 4 main spokes in the wheel of a yearly cycle.

At the beginning, in b.c.e (before common era) 20.238, the start of the First Sun Age, earthlings had the 22 star formation zodiac to help the 9 planets of the solar system for Venus only arrived to entertain us at the end of the 4th Sun Age in b.c.e 3113. The number 22 is 4 as a real number. It represents 3 + 1. The 3 + 1 elements, the trinity and the Creator Force, the cycles of the Moon, the 4 initiations, the 4 sides of the pyramid, the 4 directions and the keywords to the total consciousness of the universe. These are: Law, Order, Truth and Fulfilment.

Astronomical changes come with the constant motion of the universe. The change we are experiencing at the moment is the biggest in the life of earthlings for it is not only the quantum leap of the Solar System but that of the Galaxy I refer to by the name Kabutoreos.

A galaxy is a co-existence of star-formations travelling around a pulling power. Every energy particle, regardless of the size, is connected to a centre with a pulling power. The law of *likes attract* ensures that similar energies make up a unit. The particles near the centre have more in common than those on the edge of the unit; I would say they are more "faithful" to the basic ideas of the component. Particles on the outer circle are easily lured into neighbouring groups or by becoming a pulling power they might start up their own circle. That is how star formations start or finish. It is interesting to observe that star formations have components connecting and shining through from other galaxies. It means that stars might centre on another pulling power also. However, as energy they belong to another one. Looking at the *as above so below* idea I would say that they were swept away forcefully or they consciously stepped on the path towards change. As you can see we work the same way the universe does. We follow pulling powers that sometimes we change for another more forceful. The only difference is that our conscience can be more powerful in terms of deciding who to follow.

A cycle is a 3-dimensional circle. It shows that nothing ever gets back to where it has already been. Everything moves in a spiral which leaps into the next dimension at the end of each circle. And that is what we are experiencing right now.

Souls are not the only energy that evolve. With the constant changes the entire universe goes through many experiences. From our point of view planet Earth could be the most important. As the planet is in constant motion the influences affecting it are changing. At the beginning of the First Sun Age the planet was influenced by the 22 star formation zodiac, then it slipped into the jurisdiction of the 12 star formation and at the end of the Fifth Sun Age she arrived back to the 22 star formation zodiac.

It is very much like human behaviour. At the beginning of a cycle, we receive a key from somewhere. Let's say that we read a book. We find a few interesting sentences which give us some clue for the path ahead. We get on with everyday living, collecting information, feelings and ideas, until one day the book speaks to us again. Reading it a second time we actually understand the meaning of it; or not, depending on the experience we went through, and the quality of our learning from the past. These are tests to measure the development of the particular energy.

Apart from the great cycle of the Sun Ages and the Galactic Quantum Leap, the next most important astrological event, the Precession of the Equinoxes, is in its last phase. Human life on Earth started at the time of Saturn and now we are in the phase of Uranus. These are stages of the precessions of the Equinoxes I will talk about in the next chapter.

In everyday life we have many cycles and therefore many quantum leaps. Some of them are conditioned, like time, for we tend to have more drive at the beginning of the hour than at the end.

I would like to give you a thought that one of my students *Katalan* came back with, after I sent them to the Orion for helpful ideas on the quantum leap. She was told that in the universe past and present happen simultaneously. There is no time, only deeds. When you need to do, it is the time to do. One should consciously know when the time is right for deeds. Wait for it patiently and when it arrives, the chance shouldn't be missed. That is how time is counted in the universe.

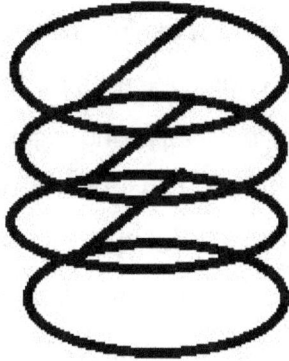

Although the people of Khem – the name of ancient Egypt, hence the word Al Khemi - understood the motions of the Sky perfectly, the 5 Sun Ages were best remembered by the Maya. Their calendar system is still the most accurate for it follows the path of both the Sun and the Moon with detailed attention paid to the sky.

The type and the force of the quantum leap mirror the value of the finishing cycle. It is a kind of stocktaking or an unspecified test on the path of evolutionary growth. Smaller quantum leaps that involve only the Self or very few people combined with the effect of the macrocosm are far less drastic than those at the end of galactic steps forward. Depending on our *eyesight* some of these events we notice and some of them pass us by without much consideration.

Ignorance has always been the downfall of humanity now more

than ever. Without observing the greater picture, we only look at life from a narrow-minded and self-centred point of view. When events are not happening the way we desire, the ego gets hurt and we start finding excuses for the outcome. According to which we usually do everything right but our efforts are not appreciated due to the flaws of the other side. When a bond breaks up you consider yourself winner or loser depending on who left whom. Even if the relationship was bad and you suffered, you take it very personally when the other individual involved breaks it up. The same consideration applies to bad relationships. Consciously you might be happy to be rid of but you are annoyed about not being the one who broke it off. It doesn't come to your mind to consider the feeling of the other person. Your thoughts centre on your own existence. And here comes the excuse: *I do not want to hurt him!* I never understand why people have this idea that it is healthy to be in a bad relationship.

Whereas in the most important quantum leap in the history of humanity we are still keeping very close to home without comprehending that most of the blame falls back on us; on our narrow-minded views towards existence. So here we are, just after the Great Quantum Leap that some of us have never even heard of, and we are still far more worried about fashion and the neighbours' views than the most important decision in the existence of humanity.

Although earthlings refrain from understanding and having a say in this decision, changes are felt in every aspect of life. There are many different views on these changes. Some of them are pushed into our minds through the media and others are triggered through unsolicited experiences from the esoteric world. Here I would like to add that esoteric is a Greek word meaning the knowledge that is open for only a small or exquisite group of people. It doesn't mean that you cannot become a member of this group. It only means that it is hard work and solely Knowledge can pay your ways.

The Shift in Human Consciousness at the End of the Fifth Sun Age

We have arrived at the end of the greatest cycle in human existence. It is the end of the Fifth Sun Age and with it the end of the Five Sun Ages cycle. At the same time, we are in the last part of the Precession of the Equinoxes. The Five Sun Ages lasted for 22.250 years and the latter for 25.920 years. The first Sun Age started in 20.238 b.c.e (before Common Era).

1st Sun Age was between 20.238 - 16230 b.c.e. It lasted for 4008 years. It was the era of Water. The Maya said that the water ended this era and human beings turned into fish. Only one pair survived.

Reading the symbols, the First Sun Age period was a very trying era for the newcomers. Due to the permanent usage of the physical body and moving restrictions, the connection to Earth proved difficult even for those with Knowledge. It was the time when the ground moved and Atlantis – Toreos broke into several parts, and shifted towards neighbouring main lands. This movement forced the people to leave the land and migrate during the Jupiter era between 19597 - 17437 b.c.e. Water depicts emotion here and the pair who survived would be the 2 poles. The event was noted and put into all the countable mythologies amongst them The Bible with Noah being the rescuer of mankind and stock.

2nd Sun Age was between 16230 - 12220 b.c.e. It lasted for 4010 years. It was the time of the Water snake. At the end, humans changed into monkeys and only a pair survived.

These symbols are only slightly different from those of the first era. Monkeys represent Freedom, Knowledge and Consciousness. It was the era of golden civilizations, peaceful existence and perfect understanding of the Unity.

3rd Sun Age was between 12220 - 8139 b.c.e. It lasted for 4081 years. Fire finished it.

It was the era of the pyramid consciousness, the understanding of the fingerprints of the Gods during the time of the Sun – Lion between 10957 - 8797 b.c.e when the Fireball was worshipped in every form.

4ᵗʰ Sun Age was between 8139 - 3113 b.c.e. It lasted for 5026 years. This was the time of fire and blood. Everybody perished. It was the time when disastrous power struggles started. Knowledge was abused and secret societies were formed to keep the Haya Sophia, the Great Work intact by hiding it from the rest of mankind. As a result, earthlings' connection to the macrocosm started to dilute. By the solar wind, Venus was turned upside down and became visible as the Morning and Evening Star to guide earthlings on their path. She is also the symbol of the occult, the hidden knowledge of the universe.

5ᵗʰ Sun Age is between 3113 b.c.e - 2012 c.e. It lasted for 5125 years. It is the time of the Sun and Fire. The planet moves and everybody perishes.

We have definitely arrived at the lowest point of our earthly existence and we took the planet with us. We turned away from spirituality and The Knowledge. We let consumerism take away our lives. We worship the dollar as the ultimate God and sacrifice ourselves and each other on the altar. Looking for redemption we join religious groups or bodies. We do everything to avoid responsibility for our existence, deeds and thoughts. Some clearing out has to be done.

2. The Precession of the Equinox

Earth spins anticlockwise around its axis that is tilted by 23.52

degrees. The tilt derives from the pulling power of its moon that makes the axis of the planet perpendicular to the equator of the Moon. A whole spin takes one earth day. Also anticlockwise, Earth travels around the Sun. It orbits the "master" on an ellipsis. On this ecliptic - equally 30° from each other, although not at the same height - are the 12 star formations of the zodiac that we use with great fondness to tell us a kind word about the future when life gets a bit rough around. During its orbit, Earth pays a visit to each star formation and spends equal time in their court. This time comes to more or less a month. The whole circle takes a bit less than a year. It means that after each yearly circle our planet travels a bit further than the starting point. Over about 2160 years these bits add up to 30° degrees on the ecliptic, meaning that in every 2.160 years Earth slips back one constellation on the orbit therefore the Sun rises in the court of a different constellation when the Spring Equinox appears. Naturally, the connection between our planet and the Sun is changing accordingly. The key date is Spring Equinox. The constellation where the Sun rises - on the end of March or early April full moon at the time of the Spring Equinox, would bear a significant effect on the lives of Earthlings therefore we call it the ruling constellation. Since the calendar does not follow the movement of the Sun and Moon, the Spring Equinox is permanently set on the 21st of March. However, Earth has been slowing down for quite a while due to its weight gain from the residue, therefore the shortened ecliptic is not in alignment with the Animal zodiac any longer. Simultaneously, by arriving back to the 22 star formations zodiac the planet closed a cycle and opened a new one; while the ruling planets of the old one continue adding to the energy field of Earth.

Below there are the milestones of the Precession cycle. I added the ruling planet and the ruling star formations of the new zodiac to the present one.

b.c.e. 23917 – b.c.e. 21757
   Ruling planet: Uranus
   Effects from the 22 star formations:
   Aquila, Delphinus and Cygnus

b.c.e. 21757 – b.c.e. 19597
   Ruling planet: Saturn
   Effects from the 22 star formations:
   Draco, Serpent, Lyra and Aquila

b.c.e. 19597 – b.c.e. 17437
   Ruling planet: Jupiter
   Effect from the 22 star formations:
   Centaurus, Ophiucus, Draco

b.c.e. 17437 – b.c.e. 15277
   Ruling planet: Pluto
   Effect from the 22 star formations:

Boötes, Corona Borealis, Serpens, Centaurus

b.c.e. 15277 – b.c.e. 13117

Ruling planet: Venus

Effect from the 22 star formations:

Andromeda, Eridanus, Perseus

b.c.e. 13117 – b.c.e. 10957

Ruling planet: Mercury

Effect from the 22 star formations:

Ursa Major, Crater, Argo Navis

b.c.e. 10957 – b.c.e. 8797

Ruling planet: Moon

Effect from the 22 star formations:

Orion, Canis Major - Minor, Argo Navis

b.c.e. 8797 – b.c.e. 6637

Ruling planet: Sun

Effect from the 22 star formations:

Canis Major - Minor, Draco, Ursa Major, Hydra

b.c.e. 6637 – b.c.e. 4477

Ruling planet: Mercury

Effect from the 22 star formations:

Perseus, Orion, Auriga

A quantum leap of the Solar System in b.c.e. 3113 shifted Earth under the watchful eyes of the 12 star formations zodiac.

b.c.e. 4477 – b.c.e. 2317

> Ruling planet: Venus
>
> Effect of the 12 star formations:
>
> > Taurus

b.c.e. 2317 – b.c.e. 157

> Ruling planet: Mars
>
> Effect from the 12 star formations:
>
> > Aries

b.c.e. 157 - C.E. 2003

> Ruling planet: Neptune
>
> Effect from the 12 star formations:
>
> > Pisces

C.E. 2003 16th of February

> Ruling planet: Uranus
>
> Effects from the 22 star formations:
>
> > Cygnus, Eridanus, Pegasus

We have stepped into the last cycle, the Age of Uranus, on

the 16th of February 2003 c.e. However, the effect of the shift arrived about 80 years before and brought us delightful fresh energy of change that unfortunately earthlings were not equipped to handle. Fear took over and powerful organizations used their material wealth to crush the evolution of humanity and the planet. As the result, we have been having wars ever since and the brainwashing power of media started to project a global consciousness with slogans we say but never fulfil. The male energy became stronger and it shifted Earth into a deadly one pole state.

With the great effort from the macrocosm, with the Galactic Quantum Leap on the 28th of December 2012, the second pole was established in March 2017 and making its way down to Earth. **The shift placed Earth under the jurisdiction of the 22 star formations zodiac yet again.**

3. The 22 Stars Formations Zodiac

At the beginning of the cycle of humanity, this zodiac was addressed when influences and the future were concerned. As the Solar system where Earth resides moved up on the evolutionary ladder, the 22 constellations zodiac appeared again. It is very logical. We have arrived at a place and time when the make it or break it are real, and earthlings still have the chance of breaking out of the 1 pole system.

Astrologers understand that something is not right with the

110

current horoscope structure. However, earthlings do not like drastic changes therefore they decided to introduce Ophiucus to the animal signs as a token of appreciation.

The number 22—just like the 12—carries an important meaning. Out of these we only mention the connection with the tarot's Major Arcanum for they play an essential role in modern fortune telling. Each star formation corresponds with a card in the Major Arcanum. The effects put a signature on the person's behaviour that happened to be born under their influence.

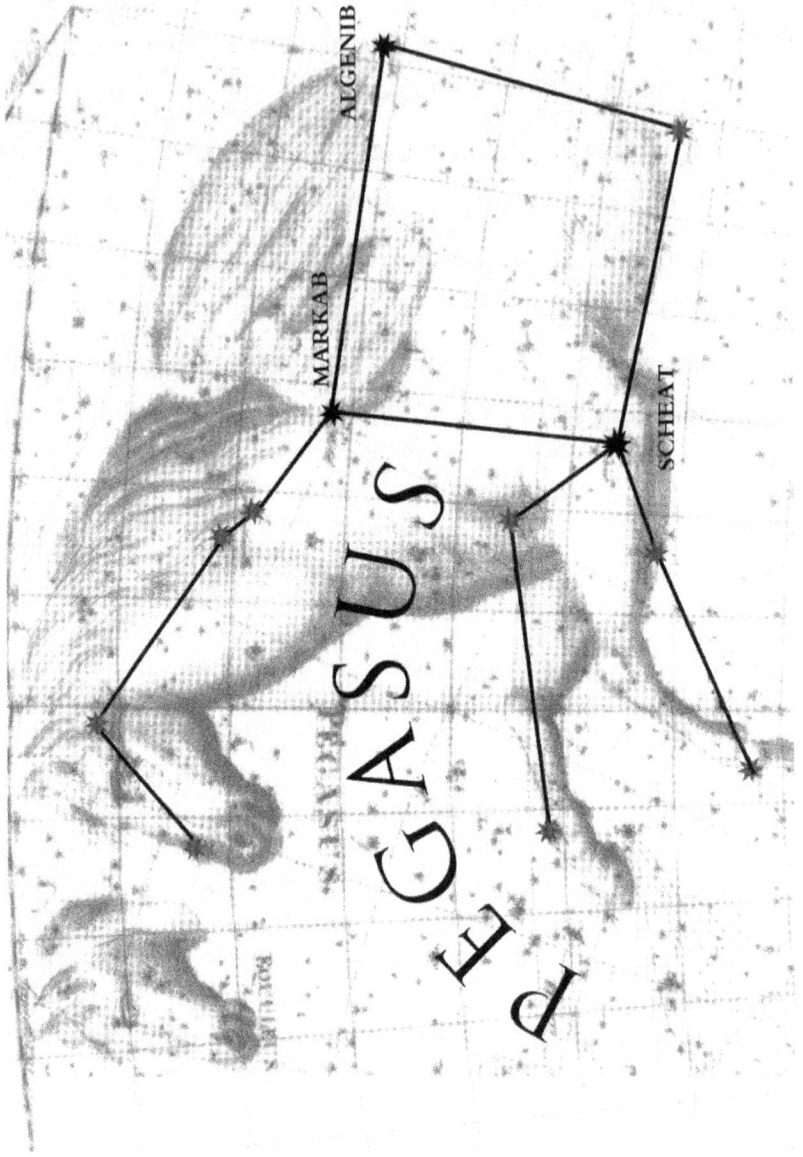

PEGASUS

The golden-haired, white-winged horse of the godly forces appears on the sky of the Northern hemisphere in the Eastern August sky and disappears in the West in January. In October it shines just above our head. Pegasus is very easy to find in the sky by the great square made up of the constellation's main stars. The saddle of the winged horse is the bluish-white Markab. The front of the animal is the enormous red star Scheat and the wing is Algenib. In ancient Babylon, people looked to this constellation with respect. They believed that it was the leader and helper of the blessed dead. In the New Age, researches proved that souls, leaving the planet, stop there during their cosmic journey.

ALPHERATZ

MIRACH

ALAMACH

ANDROMEDA

ANDROMEDA

She is the beautiful cosmic princess who is captured and chained by the Sea Monster. In her solitude, she waits for the great and courageous Perseus to free her. Andromeda appears in the Northern sky in autumn and winter. When looking for the constellation find the W shaped and bright Cassiopeia first. She is near the North Pole, and to the South of the queen lays her daughter, Andromeda. Under these two magnificent constellations is what the ancient Babylonians called the Sea. There is the Pisces constellation and Cetus, the Sea Monster who is waiting for the right moment to take the beautiful princess Andromeda, forever.

ERIDANUS, THE RIVER OF THE NIGHT

Babylonian astrologers named this constellation The River of The Night. It is one of the longest star formations in the sky, stretching over never-ending space. The river starts up at the Orion and flows down to the Southern Pole, giving earthlings the real comfort and feeling of immortality. Achernar is the last and brightest star of the constellation. It is only occasionally visible from the Southern hemisphere. It was the reason why Babylonians considered Acamar as the last link to the heavenly river. The easiest way to find the star formation is with the help of Orion. Look at the hunter's legs and to the West, you will see this flowing star formation.

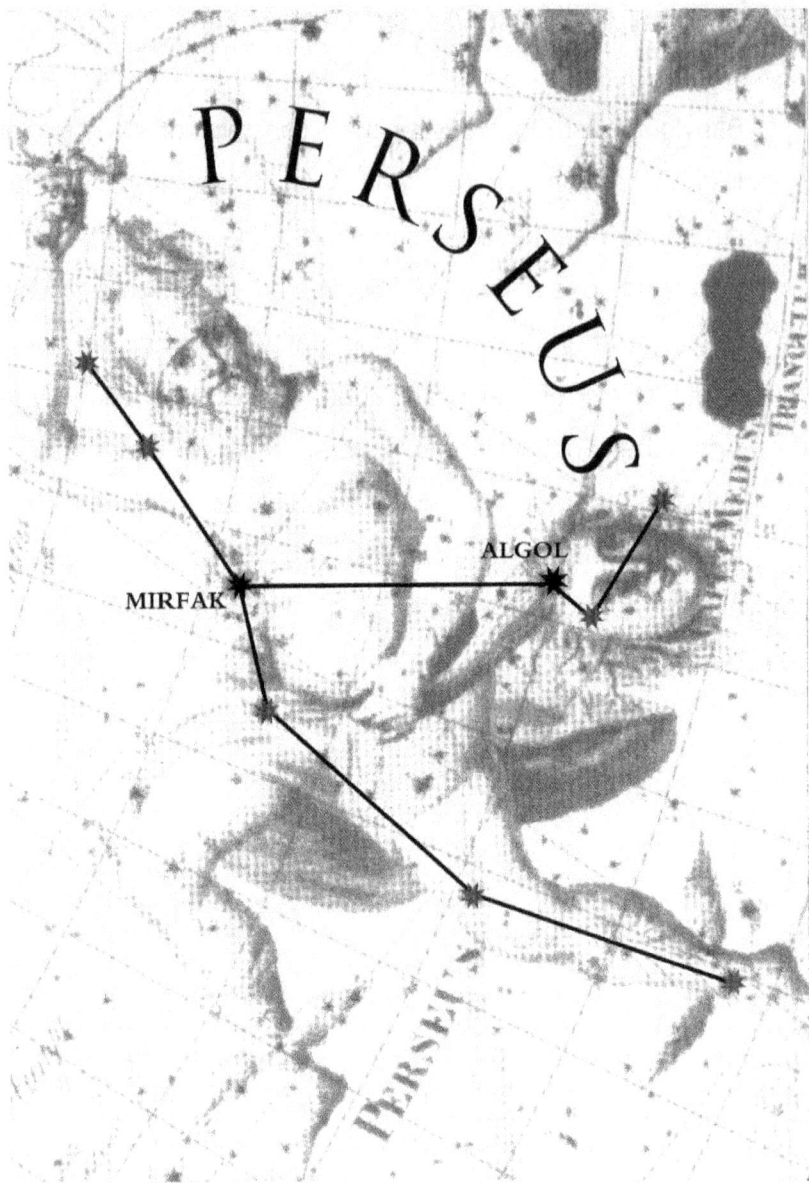

PERSEUS

The stars of Perseus are found near the North Pole just beside the W-shaped Cassiopeia. The hero with the bright armours is getting ready to free his love, Andromeda. In the sky the arrival of Perseus is announced by the scintillating falling-star flood we usually refer to as the Perseides. Perseus is fully seen in December when it is the highest and the brightest star formation in the Northern hemisphere. From November he watches earthlings on the Southern.

ORION

ORION

BETELGEUSE

RIGEL

ORION

The Great Hunter is the most important star formation, not only in our galaxy but in the universe. Apart from the Plough, that is the part of the Great Bear, Orion is the easiest to spot in the sky. It is a very bright and grandiose constellation. It appears in the Northern hemisphere in October from the Southeast and leaves us in March on the Southwest.

As he slides through the sky with the Dogs at his feet, he proves time and time again, that he was announced to be the handsomest and the best built man of all times, for obvious reasons.

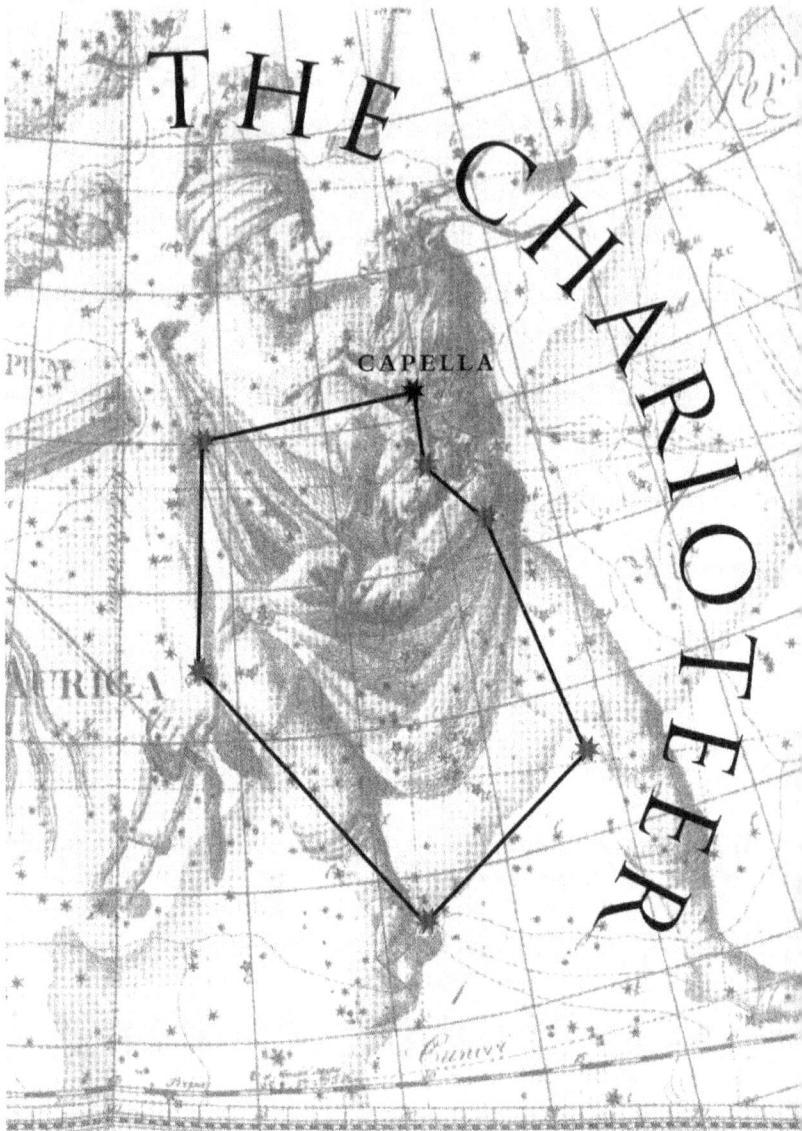

THE CHARIOTEER

CAPELLA

AURIGA

AURIGA

This great fighter, on his amazing chariot, appears to the North of Orion. Capella, the Goat Star is the brightest of Auriga's star. It is also the nearest to the North Pole. Capella is the sixth brightest star in the sky.

Capella was the star that guarded the dreams and lives of the ancient Babylonians. The astronomers of the past believed that this star brought them wealth, honour and the ability to be great public speakers or leaders. They also thought that Capella, the star with the golden beam, awakened the thirst for discovering strange fields, and possessing strange knowledge. In India, people thought that Capella was the heart of Brahma. On the Northern hemisphere, Auriga is the highest in January.

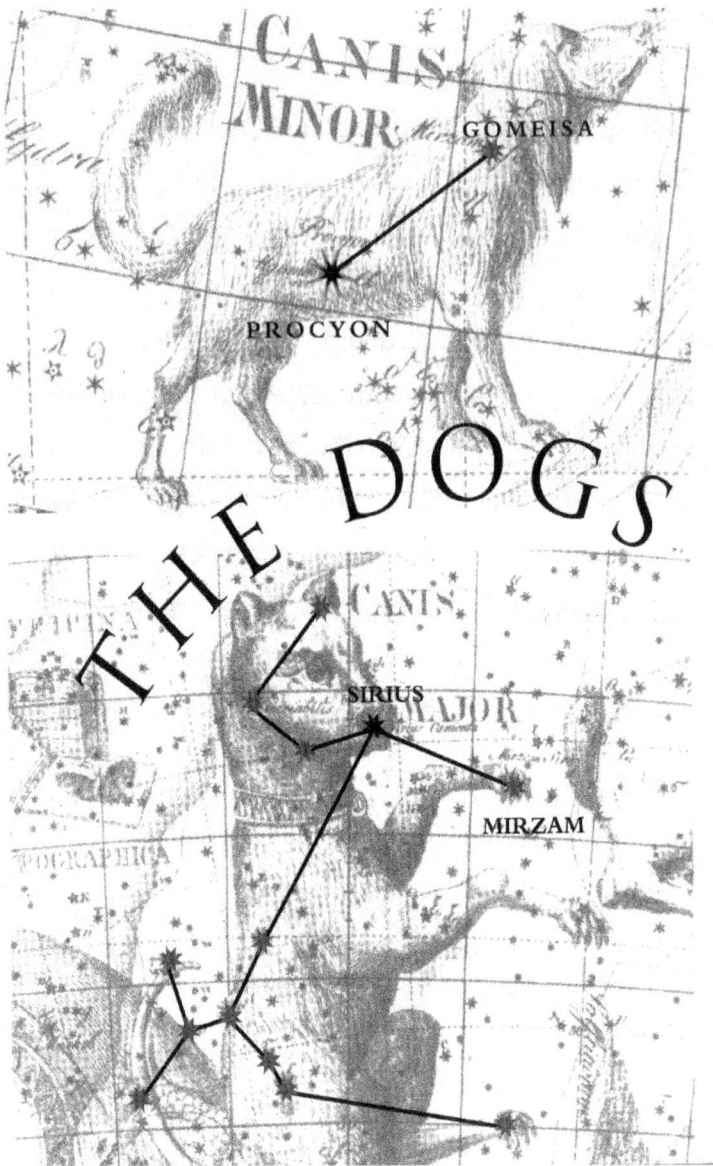

CANIS MAJOR and CANIS MINOR

Once again, I need to talk about the magnificent Orion mostly because it is a prominent star formation, it is easy to find, and even easier to relate other star formations to it. At the feet of the great hunter shines the Dog Star, Sirius. It is by far the brightest spot in the sky. Sirius is the part of Canis Major. A bit higher up from the mentioned star formation, you see Procyon, a member of Canis Minor. On the Northern hemisphere, the winter sky is the host for these beautiful star formations.

THE SHIP OF THE ARGONAUTS

CANOPUS

126

ARGO NAVIS

This constellation is far bigger than any other one in the sky. The floating ark was used by a bunch of people to accompany Jason on his trip to find the Golden Fleece. These people were named Argonauts after the Argo Navis they travelled on. The ship follows the path of the Milky Way.

The water vehicle has three parts: Carina, Sail and Puppis. Carina is the bottom of the ark. Its brightest star is Canopus. People of the desert believed that all of the precious stones came from there. This star appears in the Northern hemisphere around February. The star carries the name of a Greek captain who conquered Troy. Travellers of the Arabian Deserts also respected Carina. They named the star Suhail. The word is still in use as an expression for shining objects while amongst the People of the Sahara Carina became the adjective for pretty people.

The constellation takes over the Southern hemisphere from January till May.

ETANIN

GRUMIUM

THE DRAGON

THUBAN

KOCHAB

GIANFAR

DRACO

The **Draco** star formation is the faithful keeper of the North Pole. It is to be found between Ursa Major, The Great Bear and Cygnus, the Swan. The dragon twists and turns around Ursa Minor. Its most important star is Gianfar which represents the tail of the dragon. The other prominent star is Kochab that is known to be a part of Ursa Minor now. However, 3,000 years back it was the wing of the dragon. Grumium is the chin of the exotic animal while Etanin makes its ear. The Draco, like many other star formations, played an important role in ancient Babylon. However, the Chinese astronomers put it on a well-deserved pedestal. The Draco is still the guest of honour on the Chinese New Year, as well as other national celebrations.

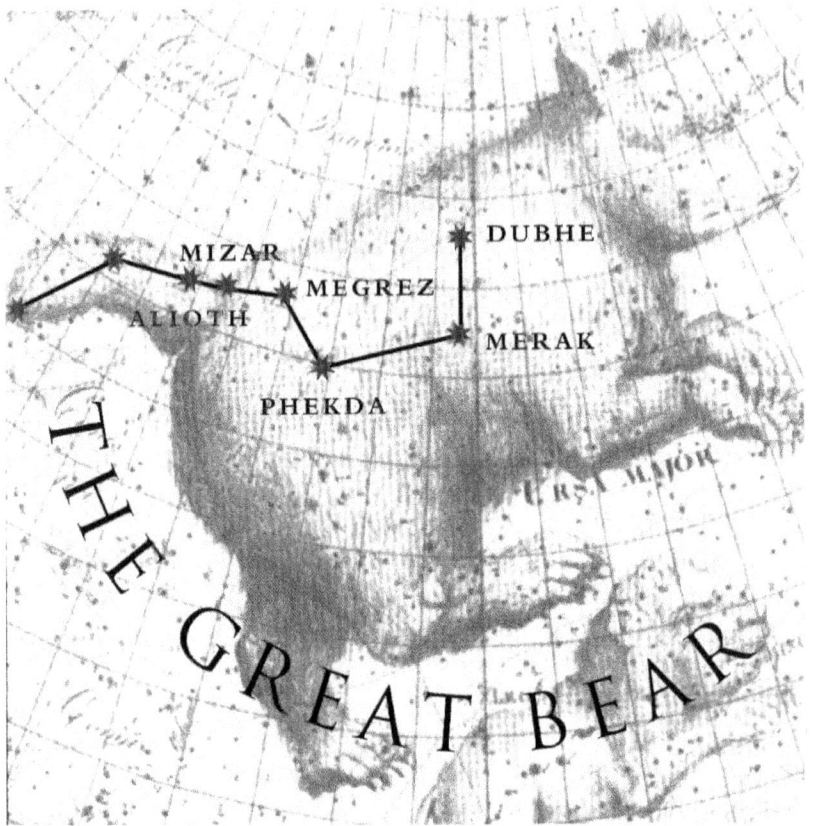

URSA MAJOR

This constellation is the best known and the easiest to find. Look for the Plough, the Ladle or the Saucepan as a prominent part of the star formation. The Great Bear shines on the Northern hemisphere around the Pole. The two stars, Dubhe and Merak which make the right side of the Saucepan, are pointing directly to the North Pole. The constellation is a favourite sight in the sky from Babylon, through Greece and India, reaching even the North-American deserts. The Greeks saw Callisto, the nymph of the mountainous Arkadia in the constellation.

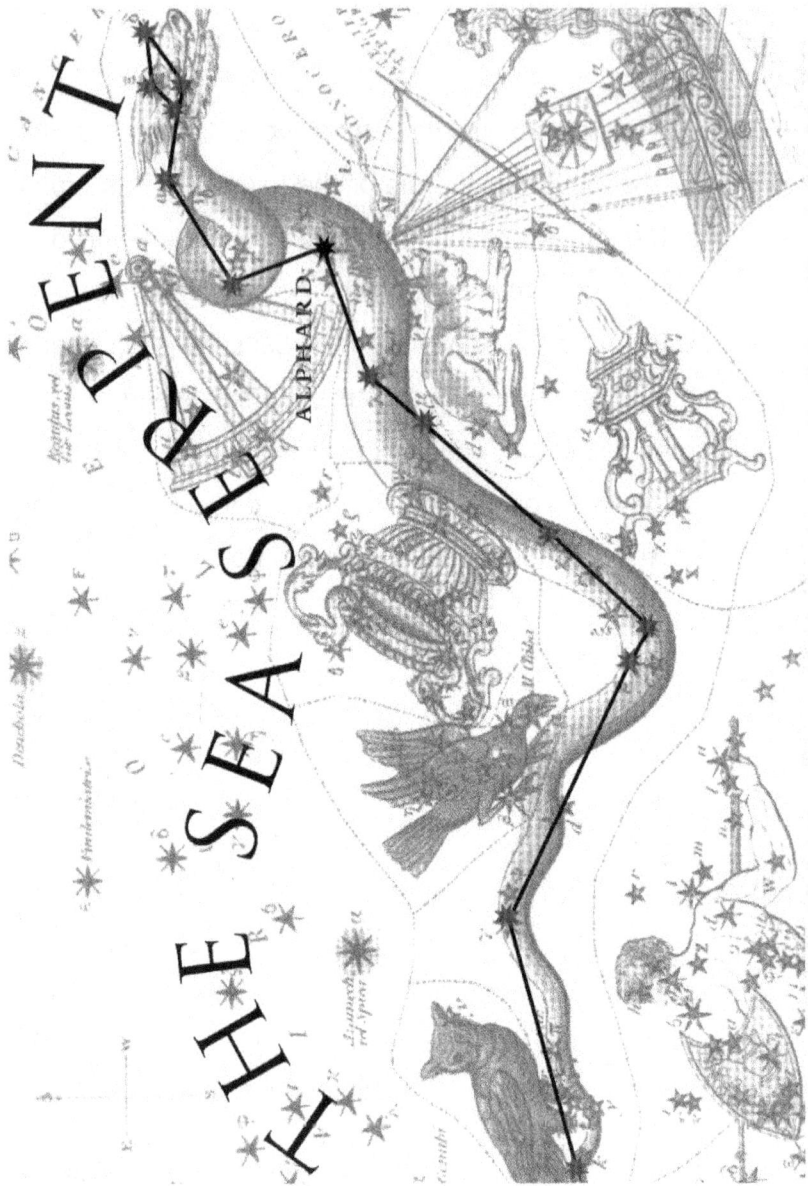

THE SEA SERPENT

ALPHARD

HYDRA

This is the longest constellation in our galaxy. The Sea Serpent takes its place from Cancer to Libra, to the South from the 12 constellations zodiac. Behind it, there are the Corvus and the Crater constellations. Again, Orion directs us to the star formation. The leg of the hunter leads you to Alphard, the heart of the water snake. This star is the one that takes care of art and music, guiding all those shows interest in humanity at large. According to ancient beliefs, Alphard awakens wisdom and feelings in people. This constellation, like many others, was the discovery of ancient Babylon. It became the role model in the frightening, female-centred society, representing the dangerous twisting and turning of the "weaker" sex. Since then, it has always been looked at as an untamed animal favouring male victims.

Opposite to the Babylonian mistrust, the Maya respected the snake-like God and was deeply respected.

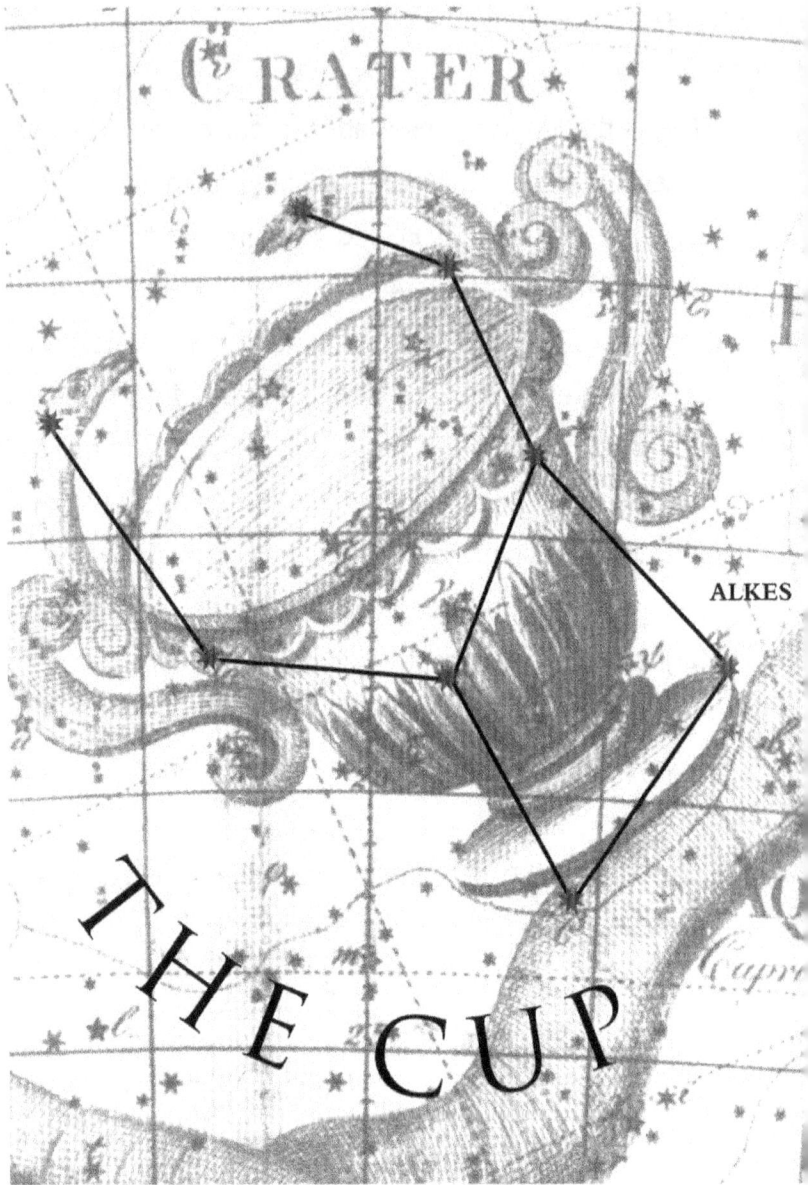

CRATER

ALKES

THE CUP

CRATER

Crater or Cup constellation is connected to Dionysos, the Greek God of wine, enjoyment and sensuality. The untamed and young god showed mortals the brighter and better side of living. The cup became the essential belonging of Dionysos and his followers. Despite all this history and heritage, records show that Greece became a wine-producing country long after Dionysos. For many years, they called the calming and soothing liquid *dark water* which takes away the reason and wisdom of human beings. The constellation is found behind Hydra, the North of Corvus and to the South-West of Virgo. Its main star is **Alkes** which is on the base of the cup. It is mainly spotted in the Southern hemisphere.

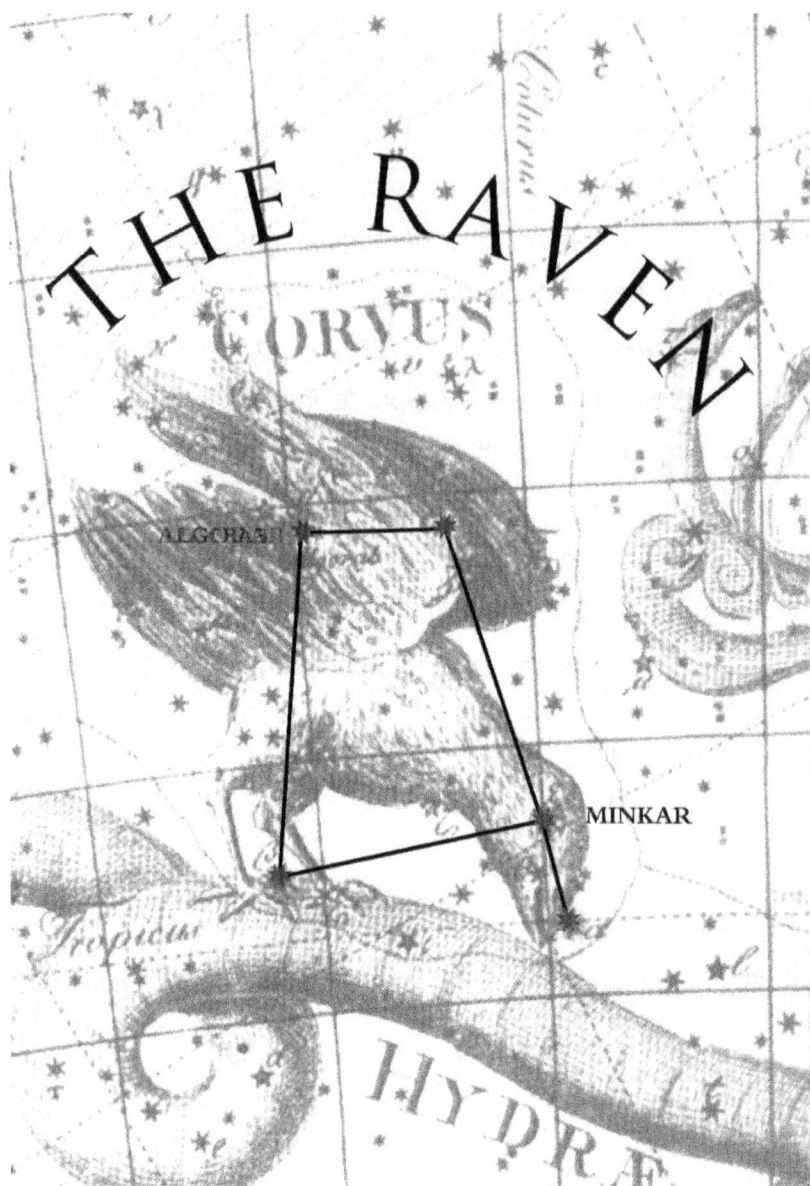

CORVUS

The Raven constellation travels the sky standing on the back of Hydra.

It appears a bit to the South of the heavenly equator and to the South-East of Virgo. To the West of the star formation is the Crater constellation. Its four main stars make up the body of the bird. **Minkar** is the eye of the bird and **Algorab** makes up the open wing. The Corvus is seen only in spring in the Northern hemisphere. However, one can see it all year round on the Southern.

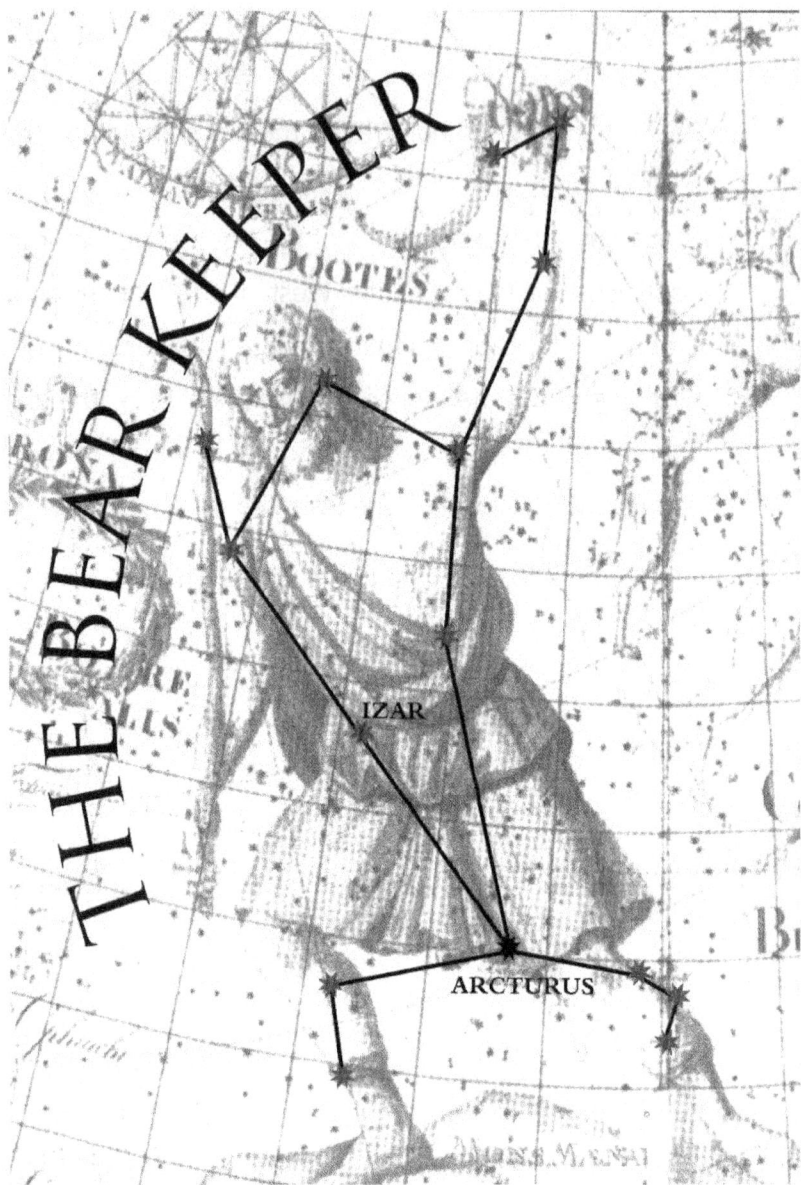

THE BEAR KEEPER

BOOTES

IZAR

ARCTURUS

BOÖTES

The Bear Keeper lies between two well-known constellations. To the North, there is the Great Bear and to the South the Virgo. **Arcturus,** Boötes' biggest star makes up the knee of the robust gentleman. The golden-yellow beam of the star travels very far. The Boötes star formation is easy to find if you follow the tale of the Great Bear, downwards to the edge of the horizon. The Bear Keeper was the symbol of the grape harvest in ancient Rome. The sailors looked at it as the forecaster of storms and imminent danger.

Arcturus is 20 times bigger and 115 times brighter than the Sun. It appears in June in the North sky of the Southern hemisphere.

CORONA

CROWN OF THE NORTH WIND

ALPHECCA

CORONA BOREALIS

The Crown of the North, or the Crown of the Northern Wind, lies upside down behind the back of the great hero, Hercules. The main star of the small, but shining constellation is **Alphecca**, the brightest jewel on the reddish crown. According to mythology, Ariadne wore it while she was the princess of Crete. Corona Borealis is a resting place for victorious souls leaving Earth. The constellation is to the East from the Lyra's **Vega** and to the West from the Bear Keeper's **Arcturus**. The star formation is clearly visible during the summer.

SERPENT

These days the star formation is divided into two parts. One is the reptile's head and the other is the tail. The serpent is the guardian of medicine and birth. In the Northern hemisphere, it is visible during the summer months. Ophiuchus, the Serpent Keeper looks after the constellation. The serpent's tail is to the East from Ophiucus. Going to the Southwest you see **Altair**, the shining star of Aquila constellation. The Raven flies on the Milky Way. **Unuk Elhaia,** an orange star, is the heart of the serpent. This star is to the West from the Keeper and to the East from **Arcturus**. It is mostly visible in the Southern hemisphere during the winter months.

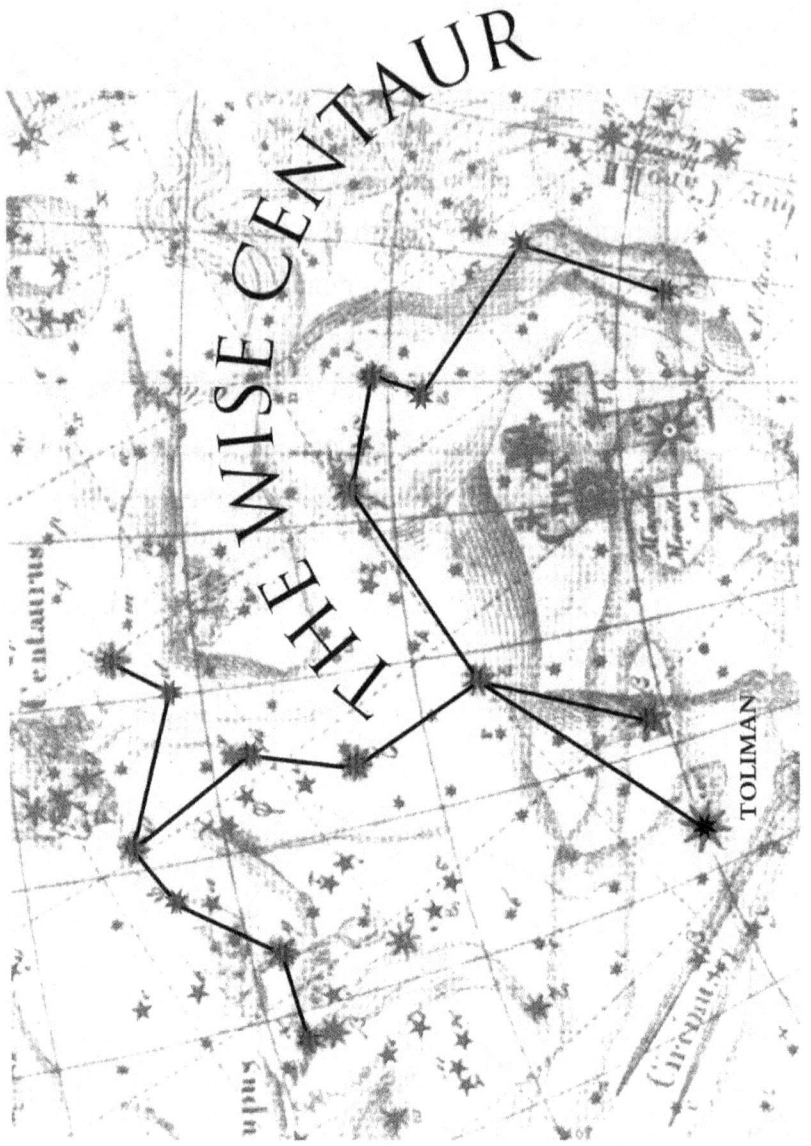

THE WISE CENTAUR

TOLIMAN

CENTAURUS

Alpha Centauri or **Toliman** is the main star of this beautiful constellation. This star marks the leg of the Wise Centaur. **Toliman** lies nearest, only 4 light-years away from our Sun. The Centaurus is a Southern constellation therefore it is best seen in the Southern hemisphere. **Alpha Centauri** played a very important role in the lives of people who worked on the river Nile. The star was worshipped it for its brightness and influencing power. It is seen to the East of Virgo and very near to the Ship of the Argonauts.

Toliman means "up to this point" and "after that". The astronomers of ancient Babylon believed that it would bring honour, wholeness and a great number of friends.

THE LYRE OF ORPHEUS

VULTUR et LYRA

VEGA

ANSER

CERBERUS

LYRA

Vega, the amazingly bright main star of Lyra shines in pale sapphire colours in the sky. It is the fifth brightest star in the visible heavens. This musical instrument belongs to Orpheus, the God of the Underworld. He played the lyre so beautifully that he enticed all the wonderful women to come down to him and say good-bye to earthly existence. Many years ago, Vega was the star of the Northern Pole. It is still quite near the pole lying at the far Western end of the Milky Way galaxy. Vega is on shows during the whole summer where together with **Deneb** of the Cygnus constellation and **Altair** of the Aquila constellation make up the summer triangle.

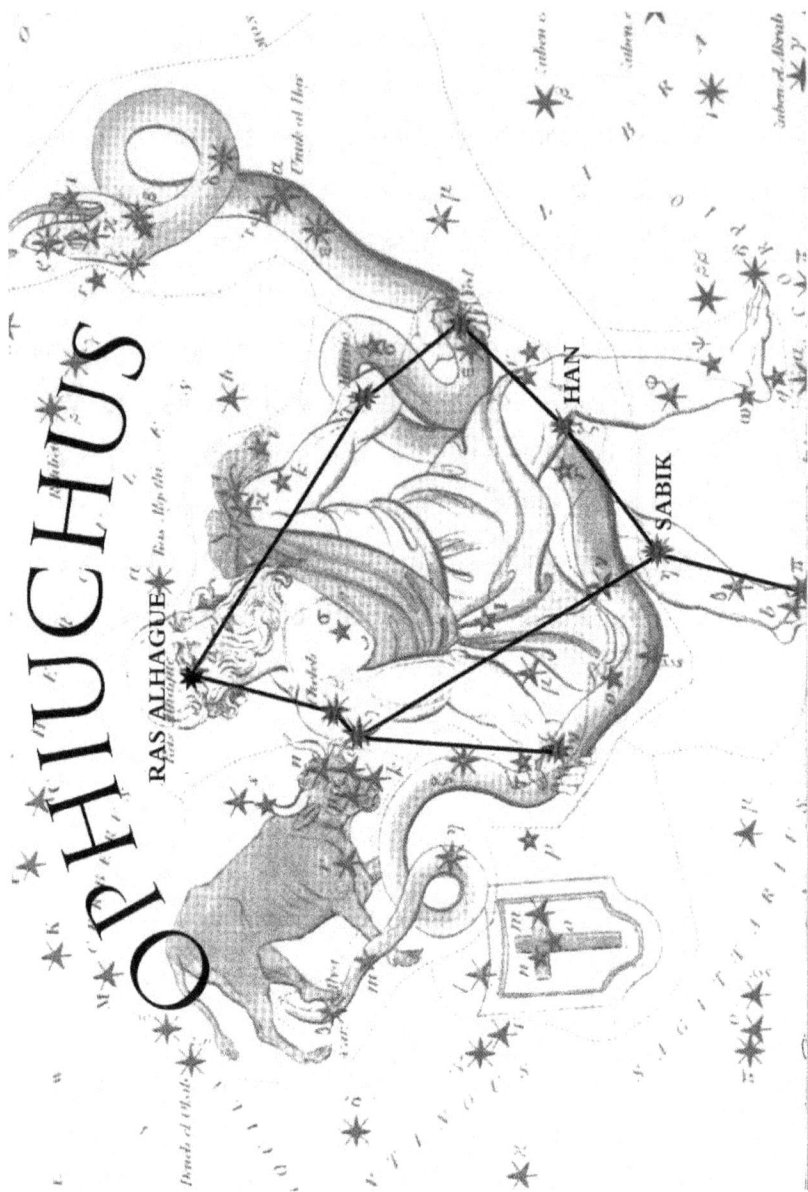

OPHIUCHUS

Part of this long constellation lies between Scorpio and Sagittarius. Ophiuchus, the God of Healing, who holds in his hands the tools of medicine and rebirth, was hit by lightning and disappeared into the Underground World. Sometimes after he rose up to the sky and continued his eventful life as a constellation. This is why this star formation disappears in autumn and reappears in spring.

The easiest way to look for it is via Vega. When you spot the bright star look south on the horizon and you'll find **Ras Alphague,** the head of the Serpent Keeper. Ophiucus helps to form the thinking of mankind. Astronomers in ancient Babylon gave the power of honourable courage and dedication to Sabik.

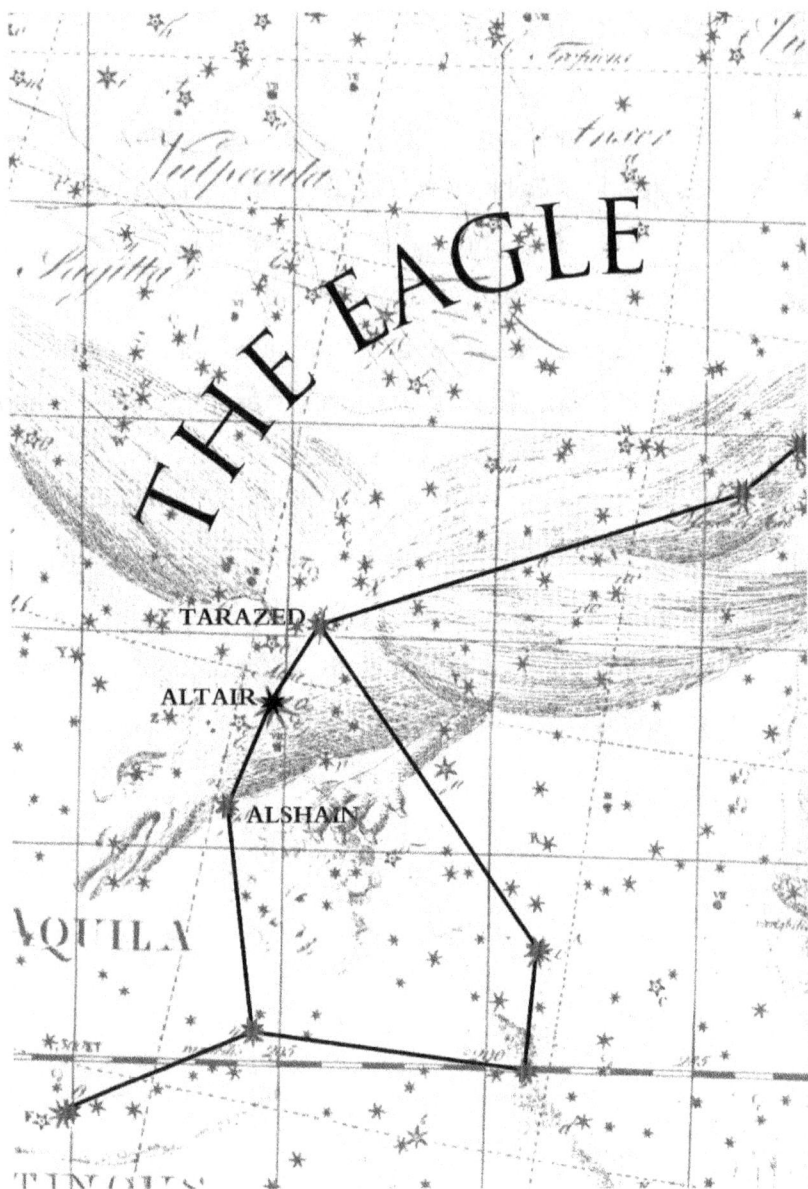

THE EAGLE

TARAZED

ALTAIR

ALSHAIN

AQUILA

AQUILA

Aquila, the Eagle flies on the edge of the Milky Way. The bright star of the star formation **Altair** marks the throat of the bird. The same star is a part of the bright Summer Triangle with **Deneb** from Cygnus and **Vega** from Lyra. Looking for the Eagle, the symbol of Shamanism in the sky, you should spot Cygnus first. It is quite easy to find on the Milky Way, as the open wings of Cygnus the Swan, makes up a cross, the pagan symbol of mankind and earthly existence. This cross takes you to the triangle-shaped Eagle with its guarding stars **Tarazed** and **Alshain**. They are on one end of the Milky Way while Vega is on the other. The Eagle is on the Western horizon from June till October.

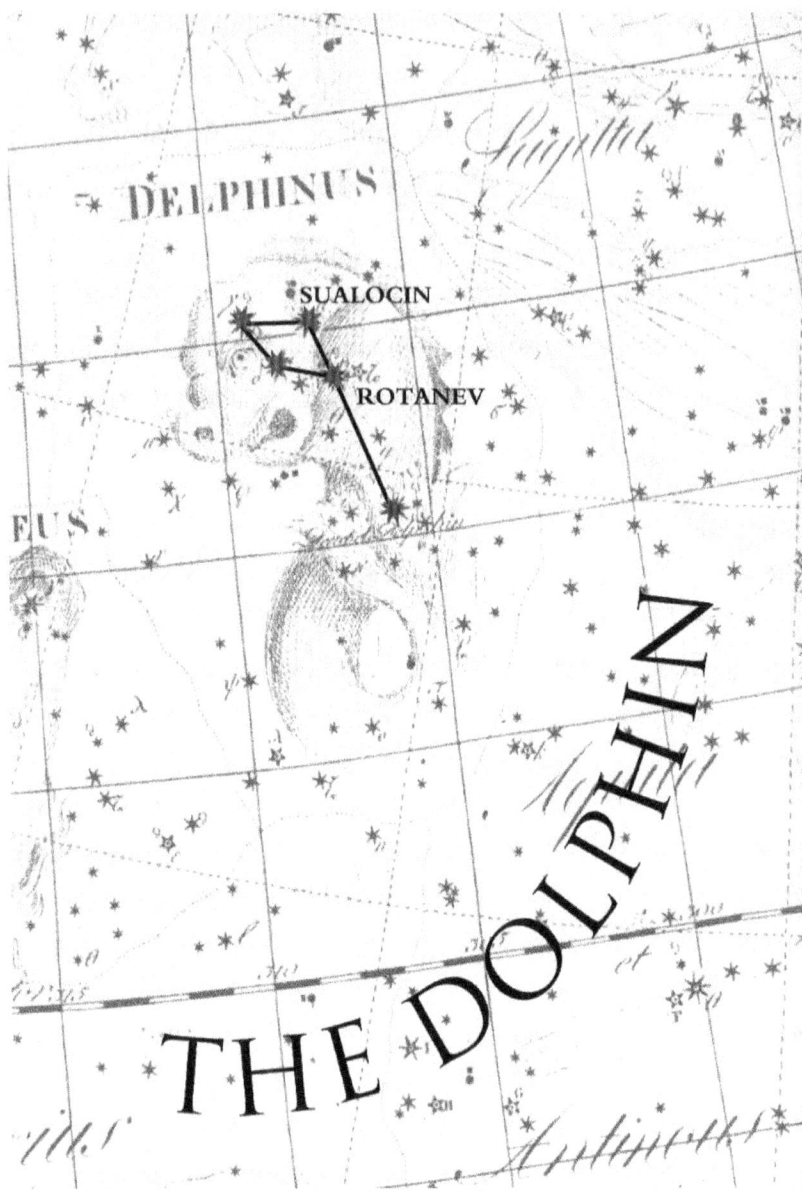

DELPHINUS

Once upon a time, the stars of this tiny constellation were called the jewel of all-stars. The best time to see it is summer in the Northern hemisphere.

The star formation lies in the "Ocean of Heavens" as the ancient Babylonians called it. It is to the East of the mentioned Summer Triangle. The main stars of the diamond-shaped constellation are the pale yellow **Sualocin,** and the darker green **Rotanev.**

The heavenly counterpart of the friendly animal had a great effect on human beings, according to the wise Babylonians. The Greeks believed it to be closely connected to Poseidon. The Maoris in New Zealand also respected it highly.

THE SWAN

DENER
SADIR
GIENAH

CYGNUS

The heavenly Swan is seen during the summer in the Northern hemisphere. The constellation is easy to find for its brightest star **Deneb** is part of the famous Summer Triangle. This star makes the belly of the bird. Because of its shape, sometimes it is called the Cross of the North.

Sadir, the dominant star of the constellation, is the guardian of smart and witty people. According to the ancient Greeks, Cygnus is the friend and guardian of the Pantheon.

Which Is Yours?

Autumn _**Mercury**_ 24th of August – 23rd of September

24th of August - 10th of September **Ursa Major**

11th - 21st of September **Crater**

22nd - 23rd of September **Argo Navis**

Autumn _**Venus**_ 24th of September - 23rd of October

24th - 28th of September **Argo Navis**

29th of September - 11th of October **Corvus**

12th - 23rd of October **Boötes**

**Pluto** 24th of October - 23rd of November

24th - 26th of October **Boötes**

27th of October - 10th of November **Corona Borealis**

11th - 19th of November **Serpens**

20th - 23rd of November **Centaurus**

**Jupiter** 24th of November - 21st of December

24th of November - 5th of December **Centaurus**

6th - 16th of December **Ophiucus**

17th - 21st of December **Draco**

**Saturn** 22nd of December - 22nd of January

22nd - 23rd of December **Draco**

24th - 28th of December **Serpens**

29th of December - 13th of January **Lyra**

14th - 22nd of January **Aquila**

Uranus 23rd of January - 19th of February

23rd - 28th of January **Aquila**

29th of January - 8th of February **Delphinus**

9th - 19th of February **Cygnus**

Neptune 20th of February - 20th of March

20th - 29th of February **Cygnus**

1st - 12th of March **Eridanus**

13th - 20th of March **Pegasus**

Mars 21st of March - 18th of April

21st of March - 1st of April **Pegasus**

2nd - 9th of April **Andromeda**

10th - 18th of April **Eridanus**

Spring *Venus* 19th of April - 20th of May

19th of April - 8th of May **Andromeda**

9th of May - 15th of May **Eridanus**

16th of May - 20th of May **Perseus**

Spring *Mercury* 21st of May - 21st of June

21st of May - 31st of May **Perseus**

1st - 7th of June & 17th - 21st of June **Orion**

8th - 16th of June **Auriga**

Moon 22nd of June - 22nd of July

22nd of June - 27th of June **Orion**

28th of June - 7th of July & 18th - 22nd of July **Canis Major & Canis Minor**

8th of July - 17th of July **Argo Navis**

Sun 23rd of July - 23rd of August

23rd - 25th of July **Canis Major & Canis Minor**

26th of July - 7th of August **Draco**

8th - 15th of August **Ursa Major**

16th - 23rd of August **Hydra**

General Golden Era Horoscope Forecast for the time between Litha and Mabon

9th of July – 5th of October 2017

The full moon at the beginning of July, marks the real summer turning point where the effects of the two poles are equally considered. After a day of ecstatic dance, the Sun bows out and slowly hands over the governing responsibilities to the Moon. It is time when Fire gives into Water yet again, creating experiences and emotional lessons in preparation for future battles and learning. The two opposite governing poles, the Sun and the Moon, do not exist separately, regardless of one's view on the subject.

All the five points on the star of the yearly cycle are equally important. I am not suggesting that they are alike in strength but they follow each other in perfect order, always adding to the work of the previous one. After initial clearing, cleansing, learning and cultivation, the time has arrived for the harvest of your work. Gathered information turns into experience, promising a level up on the ladder of your evolution.

The meeting and mating of Water and Fire are very powerful, for they fight for survival. A careless step could extinguish one of them. Translating it to human behaviour: the strength you gained in the first half of the cycle is available now to be invested in the future. If it is not enough Water gains an advantage over Fire, and brings a flood of emotional trauma putting a strain on aims and living conditions.

Looking at the energies of this particular era, it is going to be very colourful in emotions. Irreversible decision makings are on the agenda. Possibilities are endless, the only thing you need to do is start walking on the chosen path. There is no turning back! Learn new skills if you must, to add to the capabilities needed. Be persistent! The reward will be enormous! By starting to understand the human emotional structure you would get to know the Self also. There will be an answer to many of your questions.

Litha and Mabon are Celtic words, depicting the summer solstice and autumn equinox respectively. It doesn't mean that the energy cycle was invented by them; I only use them because they are well in the circulation.

Here I give you the prediction for this period according to my horoscope system.

Horoscope according to ruling planets:

Autumn *Mercury*

24th of August - 23rd of September

You are one of the lucky people who will receive love and affection sponsored by **Ursa Major.** Your relationships are working smoothly on every level and you feel wanted and respected. However, you seem to aim for more and it sometimes backfires. **Crater** speeds up events and reactions that sometimes you are not equipped to handle. **Argo Navis** supports the fear of failure and false worries about everyday life.

Conclusion: Life gives you a lot of pleasure. Take it gracefully and do not look for more.

Questions: What sort of changes can I allow into my life? How to dismiss my insecurity?

Autumn *Venus*

24th of September - 23rd of October

Argo Navis pushes you into self-assessment and to look at your life from above. By doing this you will gain a lot of self-respect and confidence. **Corvus** takes it further and teaches you to live without pretences and be proud of who you are. However, **Boötes** plants worry into your mind about the material stability of the future, and puts strain on your decision-making process.

Conclusion: Enjoy the confidence and remember the feeling when life gets rough. Remind yourself that the chosen decision is the right one, whatever it is.

Questions: How do I hang onto my newly-gained confidence?

Pluto

24th of October - 23rd of November

You spend time on trivial matters during this period. It is due to your lack of courage that forces you to stay on the surface of events. **Boötes** strengthens the feeling of insecurity and cultivates worries about the material. **Corona Borealis** would

161

force you to observe and learn. Stocktaking of life and feelings are imminent. **Serpent** lures you into a situation you are not equipped to handle due to lack of information. Finally, **Centaurus** clears the air and helps put you in a position where you only need courage to walk your desired path.

Conclusion: Without adequate information fear sets in and poisons life. Do not let it happen. Learning is a virtue.

Questions: What are my aims in life? Am I ready to pursue them?

Jupiter

24th of November - 21st of December

The power of **Centaurus** puts you into some kind of depression for no reason whatsoever. It makes you realize that your life is not on the right track even if it seems fulfilled. **Ophiucus** furthers this feeling by shutting down your emotions and makes you focus on material welfare. **Draco** takes this idea into consideration and shows you the possibilities of gain.

Conclusion: The motion of life comes from emotions. So whatever happens you should not avoid them. We have only *one life where material supports emotions and emotions make material available.*

Questions: How do I use convert emotions into power?

Saturn

22nd of December - 22nd of January

Draco puts emphasis on pleasure and indulging that makes time stand still for a while. Fortunately, **Serpent** arrives and wakes you up to endless possibilities for the future. Using its power combined with **Lyra** you should start making changes in your life. Demolish all unwanted loose ends and put closure on the rest. **Aquila** will bring back the pleasure once again. However, this will be a satisfactory and fulfilled state of mind.

Conclusion: Idle pleasure wastes your time and energy. There should always be something satisfactory to look at while resting.

Questions: How can I get ready for new challenges?

Uranus

23rd of January - 19th of February

You need to change aim in your life, for you seem to chase your own tails. **Aquila** makes you realize, that your cycles have no credit because you do not learn from them and feel stuck. Open your eyes with the aid from **Delphinus** and learn. Observe situations and people around. **Cygnus** helps organize your thoughts, creates new ideas and gives you the possibility to widen your horizon.

Conclusion: *Make an inventory of your life. Look at the past present and future. Remember, that this exercise should not involve anybody else and your happiness in your hands.*

Questions: *What is out there for me? How can I arrive there?*

Neptune

20th of February - 20th of March

Cygnus helps understand that your life is really on track and should enjoy daily fulfilment. Do not be shy to admit your achievements and be proud of who you are. The cautious energy from **Eridanus** convinces you to put your eggs in more than one basket. On the other hand, **Pegasus** sweeps away matters from the past and forces you to focus on the present and the future.

Conclusion: It is really important to admire the fruits of a well-done job. Gain energy from it and use towards the future.

Questions: Am I happy with my existence? What is my next project?

Mars

21st of March - 18th of April

Past events hardened you and **Eridanus** makes you realize that as the result you lack emotions in your life. However, **Andromeda** pushes confidence and the feeling of security ahead, and makes you feel comfortable in new situations. Through which new power is gained by the help of **Pegasus** and you are ready for new challenges.

Conclusion: Emotions are needed for living. Gain power from them and push life ahead.

Questions: Who should I allow into my life?

Spring Venus

19th of April - 20th of May

Perseus brings you a very successful period with victories in all aspects of life, supported by others around. However, the energies of **Andromeda** force you to pay more attention to your emotional welfare and channel this power towards your long-term goals. **Eridanus** allows you to daydream in a comfortable manner. However, do not forget to act on them.

> *Conclusion: Every aspect of life is important, for they interrelate. Do not stay with one longer than necessary.*

> *Questions: What is the next step in developing?*

Spring Mercury

21st of May - 21st of June

A well-deserved rest is sponsored by the energies of **Perseus.** It is an end of an era, and definitely the beginning of a new one. Life will never be the same again. The overwhelming energies of **Orion** push new thoughts of changes into existence. Finally, **Auriga** clears up situations and events and if everything goes well, it could turn out to be the most fulfilling time of your life.

Conclusion: After conscious hard work it is time for the harvest. Enjoy!

Questions: What is it I need to change in my life to fit the present situation?

Moon

22nd of June - 22nd of July

Canis Major and Canis Minor do not let you forget your usual moodiness. In the ups and downs, you find that nothing gives you satisfaction. **Orion** makes you understand that this situation is a waste of time and energy and the only way to get out of it is to look at past achievements. **Argo Navis** boosts your will-power and launches a new attack on life.

Conclusion: Being lost is the beginning of new paths. Find it!

Questions: Is there anybody with whom I would like to enjoy my life?

167

Sun

23rd of July - 23rd of August

Hydra makes you sensitive and puts your expectations high that results in disappointments. **Dogs** soften emotions and allow you to dream about a better future. **Draco** presents you with the thought that everything is possible, and you can actually take on any road you choose. **Ursa Major** gives you the courage and the confidence to back up the theory.

Conclusion: Do not be taken by disappointments! Learn from events and change your attitude!

Questions: Where is the road to take? How will I find it?

Energy shift around the Litha full moon

After establishing the cosmic and natural date for Litha, we must look at the energies we are facing in our lives on Earth.

Full Moon in Chichen Itza Mexico taken by the author

Raising Your Macrocosmic Consciousness

Looking at the political situation, I would say that humanity is losing it more and more, and real desperation is setting in. On the surface financial insecurity is to blame. However, the truth and the essence of the matter are always hidden. The surface only talks to the eyes and occasionally to the ears. It only connects to the conscious and as such, to the experience we have encountered during this particular lifetime. As we established earlier, the conscious represents Earth energies that are connected to the material, while the subconscious talks to you from the emotional, the Water aspect of the matter. The more we are open emotionally – and I am definitely not talking about being empathic in any way – the more we see the generally hidden aspects of reality. Since reality, like many other expressions we use whole-heartedly, is an illusion, my theory should be looked at with an open mind, without limitations of the physical senses and boundaries of the brainwashing global consciousness. Being able to do that is the first step towards the quantum leap.

With this desperation, the moral standard suffers and turns into an authoritative behaviour pattern. Then we supposedly have the right to kill, to wipe out nations on fabricated grounds; and we have the courage to actually praise ourselves for the deed, just because they live life differently – most of the time better than we do – or believe in something different.

This violation of free speech and free will shows that our belief system is very fragile indeed. We want to force it on others because we want to strengthen our own involvement and devotion. It is a desperate weakness due to the codes involved. Since they are not based upon the interrelation of energies, they are only wildings and designed to take us away from the really important issues.

Codes are thought forms and behaviour patterns being encoded into the energy field. Against the popular belief that codes cannot be altered for they form a genetic inheritance passed down to us by our earthly ancestors, I would say that codes are part of the evolutionary cycle and they are constantly changing. The speed and the level of the change depend on many factors indeed. Since everything is energy and lives in interrelation, the code is strongly formed by the closest surrounding. It is the family first of all. We take on family values that are shown, explained or simply given to us without further ado, paying no attention to their validity or use in our lives. We don't question them for we are guided by another code that urges us to respect our fore-parents and follow their footsteps. Therefore, their behaviour pattern and way of thinking would become an illusion of stronghold in permanence and security.

There is an even bigger influence interfering with our lives; it is the mass media, the global consciousness. Remembering that consciousness is related to earthly issues, so they would focus on the material rather than understanding emotions. On the other hand, because emotions are created by thought forms it would actually bring certain feelings on the surface; however, none of them would put us on the path to become an enlightened human being.

During the 5 prominent festivals of the Natural or Pagan Year, as channels open and communication established, we have the opportunity to make it or break it. They provide very different but fast energies in order to aid humanity. **Yule**, the winter solstice, calms the mind and body for plans ahead. **Oestara**, the spring equinox, brings fire and energy to put the plans into action. **Litha**, the summer solstice, is for learning from the experience and embracing emotions. **Mabon**, the autumn equinox, is the stocktaking of the work and thanksgiving to Earth, the Macrocosm and yourself. Finally, **Intaara Ton**, the New Year at the end of October or the beginning of November full moon, is the strongest to bring necessary changes into existence. It pushes us to the edge, where we either jump into the bottomless well of misery or stand up, allow the wind to guide and pay attention to individual moral standards.

These festivals are also the time to break from codes, as the individual way of thinking and analysing come into fashion. Although we are presented with more and more alternatives, this is not one of them. As the frequency of the surrounding energy elevates we have no options but get out of our cage and start looking at life from the macrocosmic point.

The first step is taking stock of the past, as we need to look back upon the years behind. Gain strength and knowledge from it to build our confidence and courage to invest in the future.

Make an inventory of the present. Look at the place where you are, the direction you are facing, and establish if it has any connection to the dreams of the innocent childhood. You might need to revise or redesign the path. Do it thoroughly and with affection. Remember, you are making decisions about your own life, as an individual, a path that doesn't include anybody.

When it is done you need to set your goals. They are not the ultimate destinations; however, they are needed to put the road in motion. The real value is no in the goal but in the countless experience that meets you on the road leading there.

Meditation to Raise the Frequency of your Energy Field

The next step is the cleansing of the physical body. Do it with the following meditation:

Light 2 white candles and incense. The candles need to be real candles regardless of the size. They represent fire, knowledge and the Sun. All of them are needed with meditations.

Sit down on the floor with a straight back and crossed legs. Open your knees as much as you can. Your hands should be on your side or knees, comfortably.

Imagine that roots are coming out of your sole and find their ways into the dark fertile soil. Take deep breaths down to the diaphragm. As you breathe in you feel the black Earth energy coming up into your body through the roots. Don't be afraid of the dark energy. Remember, the darker the soil is the most fertile it would be. The physical body carries all the substances of the planet. Relax and breathe. When you feel that your whole body is black and Earth energy comes out on your pores, your hair and nails are filled, concentrate on your organs and wash them one by one in this healing energy.

When you finish, you imagine that the energy centre on the top of your head opens and allows in the golden light of the macrocosm. As you breathe in the golden energy pushes the earth energy into your aura with all the illnesses, sorrows, sadness and residues from your body and fills you with the light of knowledge and life force.

Send the light back to the universe with appreciation and bring your roots back. Thank Earth and the universe for the help.

House Cleansing Rituals with the Litha Full Moon

There are certain tasks you need to accomplish around the house before the full moon at this time of the year. Again, as always when rituals are concerned, you need to pay attention to your bedroom and your kitchen the most. It comes through understanding the importance of life on Earth. The real essence of existence here is connected to those two places for the only difference between souls living on Earth and elsewhere is that earthlings do have a physical body. We are in need of it, for the feeding procedure and the reproduction of the little physical bodies. The feeding generally happens in the kitchen and the reproductive exercises in the bedroom. The other rooms in the house act as bridges between the two.

First of all, you need to clean the rooms. Naturally, it would be better to clean the whole house but if you do not have the time then just concentrate on the two.

Kitchen

After cleaning your kitchen thoroughly, you need to pay attention to the cooker and the table. These are the places of cooking and offering.

Now that the main cultivating procedure is over, we get ready for the harvest, and the larder needs to be cleaned and organized. Everything old and useless should be thrown out and replaced by fresh products. Think about your eating habits and food. As a unit, you need to produce the same meals for the whole family regardless of individual preferences. Food needs to be respected and only consumed when hunger strikes. Get rid of artificial products and time filling between meals sweets and crackers. Also, beverages have to go, apart from water and some wine you use for the ritual.

The fresh food in the larder should not be looked at as calories but as carriers of certain energies you need, to keep your body attuned with the universe. From now on earthbound living is definitely not the centre of our concern. We are stepping up on the evolutionary ladder and cannot poison our temple i.e. the physical body, with heavy and slow energy products. We do not realize but the food we eat alters the way we think and the attitude we use towards life and fellow human beings. I am certain you have seen programs in TV where they compared the behaviour pattern of people eating artificial and slow energy products with those having a healthier approach to food. The latter is more peaceful, having less stress and violence. I also want to remind you that it is not a choice anymore. We are actually fighting for survival here. It is not an individual survival but the continued existence of the human race. Therefore, it is essential to involve the whole family in the procedure.

A colourful present for the kitchen is a good idea also. A lively kitchen takes pleasure from cooking and feeding your family and acts as a channel to bring in the blessing of the universe. The best present of them all is the preparation of the ritual food that is shared with the whole universe. For this event we use certain recipes you find below. Thanks should be given at the table with the understanding that we are responsible for each other's thought-forms and deeds for everything is interrelated.

All organic energies exist under the jurisdiction of a ruling planet. As my research shows earthlings tempt to favour food belonging to the same planet as they are.

Recipes for Litha Rituals

leek and potato soup

Ingredients:

500 g potatoes *mercury*

1 leek *mercury*

2 tablespoons butter *sun*

4 spoons of natural yoghurt *venus*

1 pinch of salt *moon*

1 pinch of freshly ground black pepper *mars*

4 pinch of grated nutmeg *mercury*

1 pinch of dried marjoram *sun*

3 bay leaves *mercury*

cooking instructions:

Peel and dice potatoes. Wash leek thoroughly and chop.
Melt butter in a big saucepan, throw vegetables in it, and turn over few times. Pour on 2 litres of water; add marjoram, bay leaves with salt and cook until soft. Mash in food processor add yoghurt and serve with nutmeg and black pepper to taste.

useful hints:

When you clean a leek, chop off the top leafy part. Cut a thin slice off the other end also. Slash open length wise to the middle and wash under running water opening up between the leaves.

Elzekaria

ingredients:

1 cup dried butter beans *mars*

1 small white cabbage *saturn*

1 big onion *mars*

2 cloves of garlic *mars*

2 thin slices of smoked bacon *jupiter*

1 tablespoon corn oil *mars*

1 pinch of salt *moon*

1 pinch of freshly ground black pepper *mars*

100 g Greek yoghurt *venus*

cooking instructions:

Soak beans overnight in 3 cups of water.

Next morning bring beans to boil with the water. Add more water if needed. Remove from heat and let it stand for 1 hour. Drain and remove accessible skin from beans.

Slice bacon and fry on corn oil until brown in a big saucepan. Clean and chop onion, crush garlic. Add to bacon.

Clean and slice white cabbage and add to the onion mixture with the beans. Pour in 2 litres of water and cook over low heat, covered for 2 hours. Add salt and pepper and cook until soft. Add water if needed.

Serve warm with a tablespoon of yoghurt on each plate.

useful hints:

Bacon is optional.

Add salt at the given time. Beans cook faster without salt.

Sunday parsnip

ingredients:

4 parsnips *mercury*

2 tablespoon butter *sun*

2 tablespoon Dijon mustard *pluto*

1 tablespoon honey *venus*

4 tablespoon good whiskey or brandy *pluto*

1 pinch freshly ground black pepper *mars*

2 tablespoon finely chopped parsley *saturn*

cooking instructions:

Peel and chop parsnips.

Melt butter and brown parsnips on it. Add ½ cup of water and cook for 5 minutes. Add mustard, honey and whiskey and cook for further 3 minutes.

Sprinkle with pepper and garnish with parsley.

useful hints:

It is the icing on the Sunday roast.

fainting aubergine

ingredients:

2 smaller or 1 big aubergine *venus*

2 red onion *mars*

2 green pepper *saturn*

500 g tomato *sun*

4 cloves garlic *mars*

3 tablespoon olive oil *sun*

1 cup finely chopped fresh parsley *saturn*

4 cardamom *mercury*

4 cloves *venus*

½ teaspoon ground cinnamon *venus*

½ nutmeg—grated *mercury*

1 teaspoon paprika *mars*

1 pinch of coriander powder *pluto*

½ teaspoon freshly ground black pepper *mars*

2 lemons *venus*

1 cup finely chopped fresh coriander leaves *venus*

1 cup of water *moon*

1 tablespoon salt *moon*

½ teaspoon salt *moon*

for the rice:

2 cups of long grain rice *moon*

8 cups of water *moon*

1 pinch of salt *moon*

4 tablespoon butter *sun*

1 tablespoon water *moon*

for garnish:

½ cup almonds—blanched *venus*

½ cup sultana *sun*

2 tablespoon olive oil *sun*

cooking instructions:

Wash aubergines, remove ends and slash open at one. Place in deep bowl with 1 tablespoon salt to soak for at least 2 hours.

Remove from water, squeeze them out and wipe off access water with a tea towel.

Mix cardamom, cinnamon, cloves, nutmeg, paprika, and coriander powder, black pepper and grind together. Clean and chop onion, pepper, and tomato.

Peel and chop garlic. Throw it on hot olive oil and brown.

Remove garlic pieces from oil and put aside.

Reheat oil and burn the aubergines on it. Remove from oil and put aside. Lower the heat under oil, add onion, pepper, coriander, parsley, tomatoes with a pinch of salt. Cover and cook until soft. Stir in the spice mixture and leave to cool. Line a big saucepan with half of the aubergine. Fill with the mixture and put on the other half. Sprinkle with the tablespoon water and the lemon juice. Cook over low heat for 1 hour.

Pour the 2 cups of rice into 8 cups of boiling water. Add 1 tablespoon salt and cook until outside is soft but inside is still hard. Drain.

In a separate saucepan heat 2 tablespoons butter. Scoop on 2 tablespoon rice and arrange on the bottom of the saucepan.

Spoon the rest of the rice on the top. When all the rice is in the saucepan make a hole in the middle with the handle of a wooden spoon.

Melt the other 2 tablespoon butter in a small pot, mix with 1 tablespoon water and pour into the hole you created in the middle of the rice. Cover the pan with a clean tea towel and put the lid on the top of it. Cook over low heat for 10 more minutes. Remove from heat and leave to stand for further 10 minutes still covered.

While the rice is cooking, heat 2 tablespoon olive oil in a small pan. Fry almond on it for 5 minutes. One minute before being ready add sultanas and fry together.

Place aubergines on a big plate carefully. Pour rice onto another and decorate with the almond and sultana mixture.

You may offer pitta bread—*mars* with it.

useful hints:

Always soak aubergine in plentiful of cold, salted water to absorb the salt. Wipe aubergine dry before frying to make it crispier.
I like to use small aubergines.
The cinnamon, cloves, nutmeg, paprika, coriander, cardamom and black pepper make up the most popular spice mixture called baharat. Advisable grinding a bigger portion and keep in a tightly closed jar.

melon bowl

ingredients:

2 potatoes cooked in skin   *mercury*

1 small melon   *venus*
1 tablespoon sherry   *moon*
1 tablespoon honey   *venus*
1 tablespoon finely chopped fresh dill   *jupiter*
100 g single cream   *mercury*
12 strawberries   *venus*
1 pinch of salt   *moon*
1 pinch of freshly ground black pepper   *mars*
2 stems fresh dill   *jupiter*

cooking instructions:

Peel cooked potato and dice.

Halve melon, remove seeds, slice, peel and dice. Put into food processor with the honey, chopped dill, single cream, sherry, salt, pepper and mash. Spoon diced potato into a glass bowl. Pour on mash and cool.

Serve decorated with strawberries and dill leaves.

useful hints:

The sherry you preserved you ginger in comes very useful with this dish. Gives a bite to the blend.

Bedrooms

Apart from reproduction, bedrooms serve as a place for resting and subconscious channelling. Here I would like to remind you that electronic equipment such as television, video player, computer and others are really unhealthy to keep in the bedroom. They contain a very large amount of slow energy which they spread continuously.

From our point of view channelling is the most important in the bedroom. While we sleep the astral body starts working. It goes through dimension and time zones to bring useful keys to help

184

enhance life. It keeps you out of trouble or gives you a tip on your next move. Most of the time we do not remember of dreams due to the common belief that good

Bedrooms should have some colourful textile for this period. Air it properly, burn some incense and light a pink or purple candle.

Together with the Moon, we have 10 planets in the Haudi solar system which influence our earthly journey. Below are examples of the spiritual views related to a few of these planets.

The Sun

The beautiful and extremely dangerous fireball is the centre of the Solar system taking up 98% of the group. A turn around its axis takes 37 earthly days at the poles while due to the pulling power of the tiny Mercury it is reduced to 26 days at its Equator. Looking at the details of the motion, the power of Mercury is clearly visible:

One circle is 360°
360° takes 37 days at the poles
During a day the Sun turns 9.729°

360° takes 26 days at the Equator

During a day the Sun turns 13.846°

13.846 − 9.729 = 4.1

The ecliptic of the Sun is shifted by 7° to its equator so is that of Mercury.

The latter needs 87.969 days to complete a turn on its axis.

360°degrees takes 87.969 days

During a day Mercury completes 4.1°on its axis.

As Mercury travels on the line of the Sun's equator it pulls the fireball by exactly 4.1°. The tearing motion results in the solar wind loops.

The plasma within the fire–wind is magnetically charged and when strengthened by Uranus has an enormous effect on Keta.

In the interrelation of energies, the effect of the Moon becomes more apparent.

The task of the solar flare is to pull the karma out of Keta that has been deposited by earthlings as a result of unsolved and unfinished deeds. The mishandling of nature and its natural resources add to the karmic blockages.

From a macrocosmic point of view, every planet is an organic energy mass and as such has a soul.

There are 4 separate star gates on the Sun. They house different help centres for the spiritually aware astral travellers.

A star gateway is a space that is cut out of the cosmos by a geometrically designed form. The purpose of a stargate is to manipulate the energies within by filling it with an adequate substance, different from that of its surroundings. It is like creating an isolated microcosm with no or very little effect from the macrocosm. The shape and the filling substance always depend on the usage of the space.

In everyday life, we have many *star gates*. The place we call home is one of them. The energy within is created by the inhabitants, mirroring their thought forms, behaviour pattern, belief system, individual emotional state, health and the quality of the relationship they have within. The shape of the dwelling is also important, for walls and corners alter the flow of energy. Having separate rooms for every member of the household is great in many ways. However, they are actually small *star gateways* within a larger one nurturing individual energies and isolating the possibility of blending. As a consequence, earthlings with ample accommodation would usually be stricter, closed and unchangeable. They often value only their own opinion. Last week in Luxor Egypt I was puzzled by the houses most of them have no windows but instead let the energy of the world pour into the house through the beautifully- shaped opening.

Other star gates are the workplace, schools and community places where we change behaviour patterns according to the purpose of the setting.

I could go on and on about the subject however I only intended to explain the function of a star gate.

Mars

He is very exciting for us. In my teachings, we frequent Mars for various reasons. There are learning centres, helpdesks and above all, every soul living on Earth has a house there to use for spiritual exercises, rituals and relaxation. Everything happens around the 7 pyramids and the Sphinx. These monuments faithfully follow the interrelating data of Orion and the complex on the Giza plateau.

The functions of the 7 pyramids vary. Here are a few examples:

1. The one on the left of the belt is a central tool warehouse. It houses some of the tools we use for healing, psychic reading and meditation; for example: crystals, swords, shamanic robes, and stars.

2. The middle one of the belt is an energy manipulation centre. Souls use it prior to trans-galactic travel when the astral body needs strengthening or alteration.

3. The one on the right is the pyramid we go to for relaxing and rejuvenating bath.

The other 4 are helping centres where files of the subconscious can be opened, and energy level can be harmonized. There is one for time travel and thought organization.

Sirius

This heavenly body is part of the Canis Major constellation. After the star gateway opening in 1972, many souls arrived on Earth from this shining star.

Sirius has always been a curious subject. Its power and healing energies are legendary. Great Shamans and energy manipulators are in constant communication with the planet using its energies for healing.

Sirius houses the largest hospital in the galaxy where various healing methods are used to cure the physical bodies of earthlings. Only healers with great value and permission may frequent the place for it is not equipped to welcome idle visitors. The first-generation Kronos lent his soul to the planet.

Early civilizations from Sumer, Babylon, Assyria and Egypt, respected Sirius and used its power for rituals and events. Phoenix the firebird is the symbol of rejuvenation and the cycle of interrelated energies represents the bright star. The African Dogon embraced the same idea and followed the cycles of Sirius faithfully.

Due to its importance unsolicited visiting is not allowed.

Moon

The influence of the Moon is constant. We do not give it much thought but the axis of Earth is tilted by 23.5° to make it perpendicular to its equator. This is due to the pulling power of the silvery planet.

As I explained earlier earthlings have a ruling planet from the Solar system as does every other organic energy like vegetation and animals. This is important because we are in the cycle of nature for our nourishment and as my research shows we subconsciously favour the food grown under the influence of the same planet.

Libraries in the Galaxy

Akasha

It is a diamond-shaped star gate near Rigel of Orion. Everything connected to earthlings is there - the birth of the planet, the plan to save Earth, the arrival of the first earthling, events throughout the 5 Sun Ages, the history of energies and their effects. Souls living on Earth would find the documentations of their origin with the previous cosmic as well as earthly lives in this star gate.

A visitor's pass can only be obtained by permission.

There are further libraries on Venus, Galluba and Xerox.

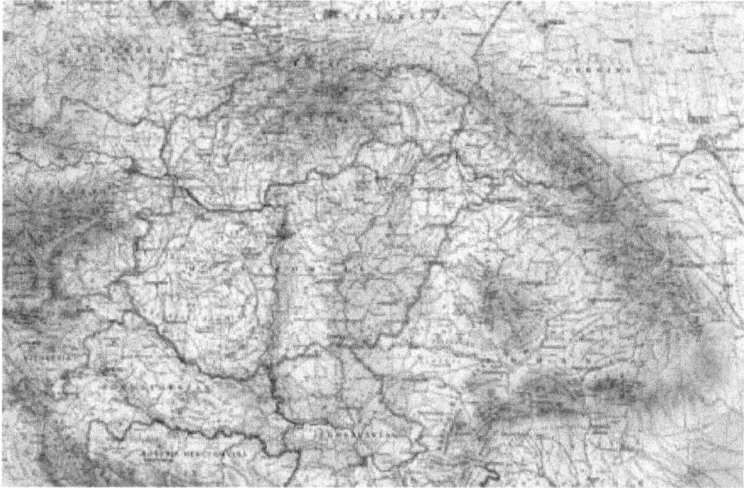

Here are the 7 major chakras of planet Earth:

Base chakra – Lalibela, today Ethiopia

Sex chakra – Nile delta

Solar Plexus – The plateau between Euphrates and Tigress, today Iraq

Heart chakra – Toreos today referred to as Atlantis

Throat chakra – Ganges delta

Forehead chakra – Bermuda triangle

<u>Crown chakra</u> - Carpathian basin

During the 22.250 years of the 5 Sun Ages, with the interrelation of energies, our planet that I call Keta, has changed. Like every organic energy mass, it also has seven major centres that are responsible for the same activities as those of an earthling. It means that the Base centre is responsible for connections and ties to all the living energies on the planet; the Sex centre is responsible for reproduction, in this case healing the wounds inflicted by those living energies; the Solar plexus centre connects her to other planets in the Solar system; the Heart centre takes in emotions; the Throat centre is where responsibilities live; the Forehead centre establishes connection with the outer world; and the Crown takes in the Knowledge and fast energies from the universe.

As Earth is in the evolutionary process and going through the necessary changes, the energy centres have shifted to the place where they are now. Nevertheless, with a substantial help from us earthlings, the planet is becoming heavier and denser while hanging onto her place within the Solar System and taking advantage of its pulling power. The planet works and behaves like us. Leaping into the future and a higher evolutionary place requires faster, lighter energies of courage and openness. They are achieved by using the unlimited help of the Fire element from the universe. However, unsolved issues, the misery of the past and present with the unconscious floating, earthlings are not ready for an advancement, and hanging onto everything they find. The principal mass energy around them is the planet itself therefore, they use the Earth element to tie them to the place where they are, keeping the planet from advancing. And Keta strikes back. She looks for the weakest link in the chain to break the self-demolishing cycle for the evolution process cannot be stopped. Eventually she needs to connect to the Macrocosm with the aid of Fire, the highest frequency element, to meet the heavenly triangle. This motion results in volcanic activities, ground movements, viruses and other natural disasters we experience right now. It is the way the planet shakes off the hindering factors that keep her captive and reaches out for freedom.

Looking at human beings, we are shifted towards lightness, to enable us to release the spring of light within. To find the Fire element, which has been planted into our energy field, the chip connecting us with the universe or let's say the Creator force, has to be activated, for that is the starting point of existence. The place of the chip varies according individual spiritual development. If you are Earthbound then it is down in the Base chakra and it rises when you advance on your spiritual education.

Old souls would find it very difficult to leave the tight boundaries of the planet therefore they would have this chip, which I call the centre of gravity, others might refer to it as hara, down in the Base or Sex energy centres. In this case the individual is tied to the planet very strongly, meaning that it doesn't care for changes and is extremely narrow-minded. They would end up with kidney problems and very often with severe depression. These are the results of never changing and refusing to go with the flow.

In this case, the 2 poles are represented by the axis. The 2 energy centres delimit the axis are connected to form a tube along the spine. These are the Base and the Crown.

We need to get back to the basic understanding of *as above so below,* and with this principle, we are able to see the whole universe within us. Let us talk about the triangles again.

The whole universe is made up of numbers. They each carry certain data. Numbers create the structure of the universe. Regardless of the number and data, the structure itself consists of segments. Every segment carries the structural numbers. Therefore, the whole is the part of the one and the one is the part of the whole. The number 10 Akia-Path-Finder says:

Only through the universe you can get to know yourself.

In each segment, there is a trace of the 4 basic elements that make up the universe. On Earth, the 2 most important are Earth and Water. They create the straight horizontal side of the lower triangle, while Air makes up the peak of it. The macrocosmic triangle consists of Water and Air as the straight line, while Fire makes up the peak facing downwards. The 2 triangles slip into each other, depicting the meeting of the 2 Trinities. This is the Trinities of the Elements.

Everything in the universe is evolving. So does Earth and earthlings. This evolution is provided by the 4th element Fire, by making its way through Air into the dense substance of Water and Earth. As it plunges deeper into the earthly triangle it brings the evolutionary point nearer; when the Fire element takes over and Knowledge becomes available.

To arrive there the ties and connections in the Base chakra need to be cut and forgotten. Forgetting means that you have learned everything handed to you through these ties and connections. If they were consciously not adding to your life, they would keep coming back to you in a different form until you understand the reasons behind the teaching. With ties and boundaries, the evolution is not possible. The shadows of the past should be cleared to give way to the light and the future.

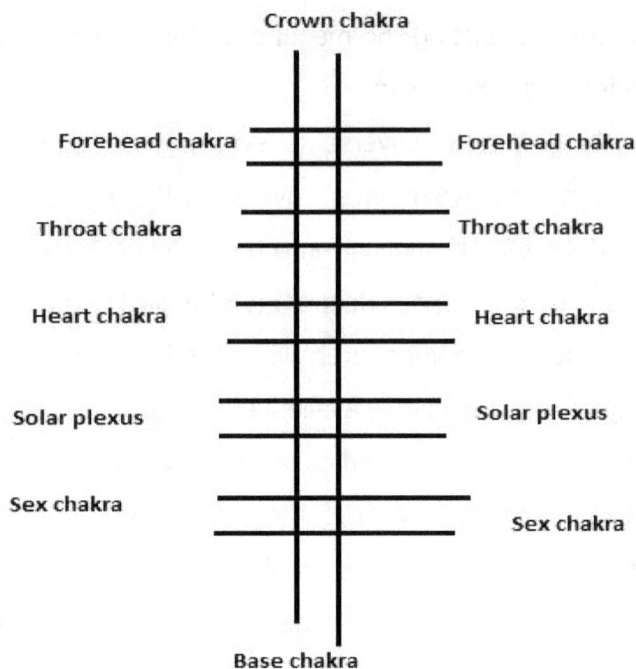

Crown chakra

Forehead chakra — Forehead chakra

Throat chakra — Throat chakra

Heart chakra — Heart chakra

Solar plexus — Solar plexus

Sex chakra — Sex chakra

Base chakra

In this process, your centre of gravity moves towards the universe until it reaches your Crown chakra where it becomes the Base of an evolved energy mass, and connects to the Creator force. The planet goes through a similar procedure. This shift of the poles doesn't mean that the planet is turning upside down. The shift happens within the Carpathian Basin where the Crown chakra of the planet becomes the Base. Ideally, it maintains all the characteristics of the Crown with its openness and connection to the universe while pulling the old Base to override it and develop into an evolved higher plane as the new Crown. The Carpathian basin is a very interesting place geologically and

196

energetically. Visibly, it looks like a brain and it has all the help for spiritual development. It is rather unfortunate that the people living in it, do not reflect that. Historically its connection to the universe was cut by different groups and the Knowledge disintegrated. The place that was originally occupied by the Magi, the educational department of Atlantis, has been fragmented by earthly superpowers who left only the small centre for the Magyars, we usually and falsely refer to as Hungarians. Although the language was put through drastic changes – first by Christianity and later by the Habsburg's – it still carries the essence of the oldest language on the planet.

6. Life Forms on Earth – Embracing the Light

Embracing the light begins the moment when the Earthling becomes connected to earthly living and somewhat disconnected from the universe for the first time. The degree of attachments is made up of many circumstantial events starting with the soul's experiences brought over from previous lives, the tasks the soul has signed up to achieve, the understanding the chosen parents carry, and the random genetic inheritance. Going into detail let us first talk about reincarnated souls.

Most earthlings born before the great star gateway openings on the 28th of February, 1972 will fit this category. To understand the necessity of reincarnation we need to talk about the souls' tasks, duties and free will on Earth.

Keta is the hardest school out of the 16 Earth-like planets. This is due to its special situation. There is the solar system, called Haudi by the Torean and also the galaxy by the name of Kabutoreos that we lovingly refer to as the Milky Way. This galaxy, the one we are currently living in, is the magma of the macrocosm, meaning the universe. As Earth connects to the Sun through its centre, so does Kabutoreos to other universes.

Once in its infinite lifetime, every soul should visit Keta for fast-track learning, which is actually intended to last the period of one's earthly existence. During which the soul lands in the chosen family with a chosen gender in order to provide the most optimal place and circumstances for growth. The degree of evolution is set up before the journey and the spirit guides are selected to aid the soul throughout the procedure. Initially, the stay planned for only one lifetime, it very seldom finishes. The souls that are not accustomed to the prison of the physical body entangles in various emotional battles and preserves slow energies as a result.

In the case of the souls visiting Earth for the first time since the big star gateway opening at the beginning of 1972 c.e. they only have experiences from different parts of the universe. It doesn't mean that they are young but never lived on Earth before. Previously souls with karma had the priority to touch down on the planet again, for karma is the unsolved state of mind that connects its bearer to a subject – usually a family member or someone close – which needs to be cleared. Souls without karma have a great advantage over those with it, for they are lighter, brighter and more connected by nature. Unfortunately, light doesn't exist without dark. Their understanding of the planet is limited therefore they find earthly existence quite unbearable. The soul imprisoned in the heavy and dense mass of the physical body loses its connection with the macrocosm and out of fear becomes attached to the microcosm of material earthly living. However, this attachment lies only on the surface.

Not having previous lives on Earth has its advantages and disadvantages for everything has 2 poles. The advantage is that without karma and prior knowledge of the man-made moral structure of the planet they are lighter, nearer the universe and better at communicating with it. These are also shortcomings. They are lighter and therefore very airy and floating. Having no experience here makes existence very difficult indeed and very often they are frightened of communication. Now that we are having the second generation of new souls the change in their behaviour pattern is very noticeable. They are seemingly unhappier, noisier, more uncertain and physically frail. It makes them much longer to grow up and to stand on their own feet – if they ever do.

There are physical bodies that do not have souls attached. I call them robots for they only use the experience of the current life without having previous earthly and extra-terrestrial life to fall back upon. In addition, there are temporary visitors from neighbouring planets, acting as informers or fulfilling their curiosity about the state of the planet.

Although they are not souls we cannot really forget about the suppliers of our livelihood: vegetation and animals. They are here for a lifetime and they do not reincarnate despite the understanding of various philosophies and beliefs.

First, let us talk about animals. Their behaviour pattern and way of life is encoded into the physical body with additional help from the belonging entity. During their lifetime they learn however they do not evolve. They are superior to humans with certain tasks nevertheless their activities are limited. Animals are in the cycle of life and therefore useful in one way or another. Sadly enough today most animals live in captivity unable to use their encoded abilities. Throughout the years, earthlings have taken away every bit of dignity they had in their natural environment.

Vegetation is essential for the livelihood of humanity, the animal kingdom and other organic energies on the planet, for it is the only organic energy that is able to take in the Light from the macrocosm that none of the animals or human beings is designed to do. I am aware of the claim amongst earthlings of feeding on light. However, it never turned out to be entirely true for it cannot be. Our connection to the Fire of the universe is through vegetation. Without them, all life forms would perish.

They have the highest energy frequency and can communicate with the macrocosm through their natural communication channel between the 2 planes easily.

We are made to believe that earthlings are the most intelligent energies on Keta. However, trees overwrite this theory. They are great communicators and mediums, healers, guides and are mostly responsible for balancing the energies on Keta. Without their work we would not have enough oxygen to breathe and the physical body would give up. Everything they do is conscious, unlike the deeds of earthlings.

When not re-arranged by earthlings they live in groups. Within the group, there is a Father and a Mother tree with the highest knowledge and certain responsibilities assigned to them. After the death of these trees, the group chooses new leaders. The leaders assign certain tasks to the members of the group. According to the task given a tree could be a:

- Sentinel
- Communicator
- Library
- Soul despatcher
- Star gateway keeper
- Healer
- Informer

The trees communicate with each other and other groups in order to harmonize their tasks. The vibration they release is detected from far on the planet. When trees fall in the tropical forest of Amazon those in Canada sense their cries.

I have to mention here that cutting trees in the Amazon is unnecessary for Brazil has vast uncultivated land, lying idle because they are properties of certain people who do not provide work on their lands to feed the less fortunate. As a result, people are forced to *steal* fertile grounds from wherever possible. However, the really important factor behind the tree-cutting mission in Amazonia is curiosity and fear.

Similarly to earthlings, trees have souls. Tree-souls are immortal. However, they do not evolve and therefore do not multiply. Different types of trees need specially trained souls to look after the tree and help the work. Tree-souls live inside the tree. Without souls, trees are not complete and their livelihood fades away.

With my students, we have tree healing missions when we find new souls for abandoned trees or change them if necessary.

There are different ways to communicate with trees. To start with go to a tree you feel connected to. Sit down in front of it and ask permission for connection. When your intuition says yes, start asking the questions you seek answers to. Take the very first that comes to you.

7. The 4 Basic Elements – Initiations

On the evolutionary path, the understanding of the 4 basic elements is a must. They are assigned to the 4 steps of the ladder, the 4 sides of the pyramids and the fourth dimension.

Earth represents Earthly living, the physical body, material, human connections and ties, inherited ideas and moral standards. Essentially it is everything that should be strongly reconsidered and reorganized to make the second step available.

Water as the second step represents the emotions you are only able to unleash once you have understood the first step.

The third is Air which is between the micro and macrocosm lifts the soul up to the blending point where the 2 triangles meet. Communication skills should be learned here as well as introductions to the different entities in the universe.

The fourth element is Fire. It represents the Great Knowledge and the subconscious.

We run 4 days initiation camps where through exercises you are connected to the elements within, step by step and one at a time to put you on the physical, the emotional, the spiritual and the holistic plane.

I enclose here 4 meditations you might want to do at home at your convenience in order to get in touch with the 4 elements within.

EARTH MEDITATION

Sit down on the ground, with your back straightened and legs crossed. Open your knees as much as you can; your arms comfortably beside you or on the knees. Relax.

Breathe slowly and deeply from above through the top of your head. Bring the air down along the spine.

One-two-three-in and one-two-three-out. One-two-three-in and one-two-three-out.

As you are sitting there, imagine that roots are coming out of your sole. Very thin, little roots searching for a channel in the ground. You greet the insects in your way, chat with worms and respectfully lower your head in front of the hard rocks while walking around them. You are searching for water and nourishment. The deeper you get, the thicker you become.

When the roots reach 25 metres under the ground, imagine the black healing energy to shin up from Mother Earth. Do not be afraid of colour black. Remember, everything comes from earth, and the most fertile soil is black. As you inhale the energy spreads into your body further, tickles your sole and caresses your feet. Runs up on the shin and reaches the knees. You see your body losing its original colour gradually and absorbs the black hue of earth, healing your organs and cleansing your digestive system, soothing the ailing points in your body. Cleans your throat, your tonsils and teeth. Your hair and your nails are all black now and gradually you bland into the energy of the beginning and the end.

You understand that grew out of it and now you want to be part of this magic. Through Mother Earth, you become life-giver and life-healer. Your physical body disappears. You are only a small heap of dust that enjoys the warmth of the beaming sun. After a while, the warmth turns into burning. You are thirsty. You need water to survive. You struggle for a movement, gasping for air, weak and almost motionless.

The rain starts up. Slowly open your arm and your whole body, your soul to take in more and more from the life-giving force.

As the rain gets heavier and the drops grow, you find it more and more difficult to hold your form and energy together.

You give up the fight. Merge with the water and through the field happily, enjoying the power of the double life-force working in unity.

The rain stops. The Sun comes out again and caresses your scattered body parts. Helps you gather them. First, your head emerges from the ground, your upper body, your arms and finally your legs. Bring your roots back, thank Mother Earth for the healing and the exercise and come back to your earthly existence.

WATER MEDITATION

Sit down on the floor with a straight back and legs crossed. Open your knees as much as you can. Your arms on your side or your knees, comfortably.

Relax.

Open your crown chakra, that is above your head and take a

slow and deep breath. Down into the diaphragm.

Imagine that the energy above your head becomes a thick silver prism of light. As you breathe in the prism reaches the end of your spine, the Root chakra at the caudal vertebra to create a wonderfully glowing cleansing and healing connection between your energy centres. Slowly release the air from your lung. As you do it slowly, feel the oxygen reaching even the smallest corner of your body making you feel hot. One-two-three-in and one-two-three-out. One-two-three-in and one-two-three-out.

Keeping the breathing rhythm, crouch with your head at the knees, imitating a drop of water. Then stand up and stretch, try to reach the sky. Crouch again and stretch. As you repeat the motion a few times, you feel the sensation of growing. Your belly grows your chest and your buttocks. The movements get slower and the drop longer. You cannot hold it together anymore. The drop starts its journey. It collects the smaller drops on the way. It waters the trees, offers a drink to the birds and caresses the bathing animals.

Grows and grows, running on the road faster and faster. It gets wider and deeper, searching for a safe channel. It washes away the dirt and the trees, moves the rocks.

The Sun comes up. Playfully caresses the water, dances on the waves. The exercise makes him thirsty. Drinks from the water and continue the movement. The beams want more and more water. The dance fastens and you get smaller. Animals cannot drink from you anymore. You are stranded. Every move hurts.

Crouch and offer yourself to the universe.

Send back the silver energy, thank for it, and come back to your earthly existence.

AIR MEDITATION

Sit down on the floor with a straight back and legs crossed. Open your knees as much as you can. Your arms on your side or your knees, comfortably.

Relax.

Open your crown chakra, that is above your head and take a slow and deep breath. Down into the diaphragm.

Imagine that this air turns into a thick and dense pink prism of light.

As you inhale the prism slides down and reaches your Root chakra at the end of your spine, producing a bright, cleansing and healing connection between your energy centres.

Slowly release the air. Inhale and exhale, and inhale and exhale. One-two-three-four-in, one-two-three-four-out and one-two-three-four-in and one-two-three-four-out.

Keep the rhythm. Feel the light slowly filling your whole body until you become a dense and pink energy mass. Your legs disappear, your hands disappear, your thighs, your arms, your lower body and your upper body. You have no head anymore. Only the beam of pink energy exists.

You keep the rhythm still, feel and see that the pink energy starts blending into the endless universe. As you become lighter you start floating and get nearer and nearer the universe. Gradually you become one with the whole. Transparent, mysterious, invisible and impenetrable. You are in everything. The whole Earth has you to thank for its life. You are the breath, the life-force, the Creator. You are the Everything, and the Nothing.

Enjoy existence. Start moving. Look around in your empire. Caress the people and enjoy their smile. Lift the hair of the girls and let it fall back slowly. Talk to the leaves and listen to what they say. Tousle the water and push the sails. Help the bird to fly.

You feel stronger and stronger. People tremble from your strength and girls chase after their hair. Leaves rattle as they try to hold onto the bond of living.

Birds give up the fight. Waives pull people into the abyss. Sails are torn, and boats turn over. The fight for survival starts. You sweep everything out of the way. Threes are forced out of the ground, Houses lose their roofs, and some even collapse under your strength. You do not consider anything and anybody anymore, only the force exists. Only you exist. The greatest, the mightiest, the life and the death.

The sky darkens. A lightning dances at a distance. The sound of thunder reaches you. Then the lightning gets nearer and forces you to slow down. Suddenly it hits you. You weaken.

Continue the breathing rhythm, slowly and deeply. As you calm yourself down, your body changes back into the pinkish energy mass.

You are a beautiful, glaring pink light. As you slow yourself further, feel the weight of your head. Gradually your body regains its original form.

Send the energy back to the universe and thank it for the help.

Come back to your earthly existence.

FIRE MEDITATION

Sit down on the floor with a straight back and crossed legs. Open your knees as much as you can. Your arms on your side or your knees, comfortably.

Relax.

Open your crown chakra, that is above your head and take a slow and deep breath. Down into the diaphragm.

Imagine that this air turns into a thick and dense golden prism of light.

As you inhale the prism slides down and reaches your Root chakra at the end of your spine, producing a bright, cleansing and healing connection between your energy centres.

Slowly release the air. Inhale and exhale, and inhale and exhale. One-two-three-four-in, one-two-three-four-out and one-two-three-four-in and one-two-three-four-out.

Open your heart. As you exhale release the golden energy

through this open gate. See the end of the golden energy prism disappearing in the distance.

This is the path. The path you need to follow.

Step out of your heart and follow the road. You arrive at a meadow. Observe the vegetation, the plants, the flowers, butterflies and insects. Talk to them. Question them about their lives. Continuing your path you reach a creek. There is a bridge over the water. Step on it, lean over and look at your reflection. Continue on the path until you reach 17 steps going downwards. Every step is different in colour. As you walk down, stopping on each step, absorb the colour, let it fill you, let it heal you and let it take you to another dimension.

At the end of the 17th steps there is a very nice spacious clearing. A campfire is lit. Sit down next to it make friends with the fire. Slowly take your clothes off, enjoy the warmth and the soothing softness of the flames. Stretch your arm and take a handful from it. Feel the fire on your skin. Play with it.

Put it into your solar plexus. Let it light up in your body and allow it to lift you up and take you away.

The playful flame looks for life-force. It touches everything around. Burns the grass, the bushes. As its appetite and needs grow, it takes a bite from the forest. There is no stopping now. The flame becomes fire and fights for its existence. Wants more and more. Its power is growing constantly. Becomes mighty and unstoppable.

Suddenly it starts raining. Plich-plach, plich-plach. As the raindrops grow, you feel your power slowly fading away.

Pay attention to your breathing. One-two-three-in and one-two-three-out. One-two-three-in and one-two-three-out.

The rain becomes a waterfall. You collapse under its weight.

Pull the path back to your Heart chakra. Send the light energy back to the universe, thank it and come back to your earthly existence.

3rd Secret: Creation and Exodus

1. Atlantis, The Cradle of Humanity

With due respect towards the different beliefs about creation, this is the only one I find feasible. With the universe being in constant motion and with the interrelation of energies human beings couldn't spring out of Earth. They had to come from somewhere.

Although Darwin's idea of evolution works within each group of organic energies - vegetation, animals and human beings - the only link between them is the structure of the universe they all carry. The mutation affects humans the most; especially since the introduction of Uranus energies the physical, mental and spiritual changes bring surprises to modern sciences like medicine and psychology.

Before The Descend thorough research was conducted to design a suitable physical body for the newcomers. By that time Earth had reached an advanced evolutionary stage regarding that of animals and vegetation.

The vast island occupied the great majority of the Southern-Atlantic Ocean between the African continent and the narrow strip of the Andes. By its local name, Toreos provided good ground for the new-comers and proved best at maintaining a connection with the universe. Its land was fertile, there was

212

fresh water in abundance and the purest of substances available on the planet.

The 144 souls dressed in physical bodies started the revolutionary life of humanity. There were 12 groups, each with 12 members: 6 males and 6 females. Each group appointed a leader to represent them in the committee.

The groups had superior knowledge of different aspects of earthly life. These were:

1. Astrology

They worked with stars and planets, observed the macrocosm and its effects on human lifeform.

2. Numerology

The duty of this group was to number different energies, thought forms and deeds.

3. Agriculture

The necessity of eating and preserving the quality of energy presented this group with ample work.

4. Stock keeping

As part of the diet and help around the household, animals were classified and labelled.

5. Communication skills

The invention of sounds and the classification of their effects were amongst the duties of this group.

6. Writing
They invented the first letters in harmony with the sound.

7. Waters and Seas
They worked with lakes, rivers and seas.

8. Educators
They were responsible for preserving the knowledge and making it available to all.

9. Healers
They kept the physical bodies in shape.

10. Energy manipulators
They observed the interrelation of energies and initiated necessary changes.

11. Astral travellers
They taught the usage of the astral body and time travel.

12. Mechanics
They knew everything about machinery and built new ones.

By the time Jupiter became the ruling planet under the watchful eyes of Zeus the people of Atlantis were ready to spread their wings and establish communities all over Keta.

The migration took the path on both sides of the Mediterranean Sea leaving tracks in Morocco, Spain, the Carpathian basin, Libya, Greece and established a long-lasting and prosperous community on the plateau between the Tigress and Euphrates. However, the aim was the Giza plateau where the pyramid complex aided the start of the new life. At the beginning of the 3rd Sun Age due to the disasters at the end of the previous one, the migration extended to Asia most notably in the Ganges valley and around the Himalaya. Egypt became an important centre where knowledge is still preserved in the buildings.

The land of Atlantis broke up and shifted apart. A great majority of Brazil is on the Toreos land, as are all the Caribbean islands and Cuba with the Southern part of Mexico. Some people from Atlantis ended up in those countries and established their cultures based on the knowledge they remembered. Incas, Maya and Quenchas still have traces of the Glorious Toreos.

2. The Heavenly Hierarchy

The Creator is the first knowledge that was able to multiply by division.

It is not a human being, nor does it have a human form, but it is the essence of the universe. A substance that carries a portion of everything, and from which everything derives. Since we come from the Creator, we also carry the essence of the universe. The difference is in the experience. The Creator force is pure essence and its particles are not soiled by experience. It is the perfect laboratory of number 10 on the Tree of Life, the alchemical workshop. People approaching the subject through the Jewish Kabbala would call it Malkuth. However, Al Khemi literarily means the matter of Egypt being Khem the ancient name of the land with black and fertile soil.

During the evolution of the soul, we are constantly cleansing ourselves to arrive at that pure state. Nevertheless, there is a Catch 22 here. We need to go through experiences to learn how to cleanse, while experiences soiling us. It is a constant rhythm of up and down until we would become one with the Creator.

At the beginning of its work, the Creator projected itself out and made 9 males and 9 females what we call the first-generation. They are diverse, symbolizing different behaviour patterns and abilities. Every soul comes from one of the first-generation couples. One's origin can be figured out with the soul number.

According to the data they carry, I named these souls. Not surprisingly some of the names are known from different mythologies. This is what I came up with:

1.   Enoch – Kiris

2. Mekai – Aurora
3. Zeus – Hera
4. Enkki – Zinas
5. Uriel – Qula
6. Hades – Ariadne
7. Mardouk – Shamir
8. Kronos – Penka
9. Uranus - Phoenix

Twelve souls of the First Generation form the Alpha & Omega council that pioneers the place. In addition, there are the 12 members of the Magi Council who look after spiritual development and energy manipulation.

3. Crop Circles and the Fingerprints of the Gods

Souls volunteered or were sent down here to save Earth from its predicted doom at the end of the 5th Sun Age. The drastic change of energy is due to the motion, which forces the old and tired planet to slow down in its movements. Injecting conscious organic energies into the form of earthlings seemed like a good idea at the time. By getting rid of the residues of the past with proper cleansing and life elixir intake, the planet lightens up and moves faster on its extended orbit. It was a necessity in order to avoid the fatal crash with planet Niburu or Mardouk as also remembered. The reward for the work was the opportunity to jump a few steps on the evolutionary scale with the hope of multiplying. And the Galactic Quantum Leap took place.

In the beginning Knowledge was clear, communication channels were open between Toreos and the Syon centre on Orion, and the energy level of the place was rising. However, by the end of the 1st Sun Age migration started and the abandoned Toreos was torn apart by a major shake. The Knowledge faded into the background and communication channels jammed. Further into the next Sun Age earthlings were pushed to remember the Great Work and the Haya Sophia yet again.

In the motion of life, ups and downs are inevitable. The 2 poles are in a constant argument in order to push each other over the comfort zone and look for new experiences. The scale of the pushing motion depends on the courage of the opposites. Courage comes from different sources. It might be from strong conviction or desperate insecurity. As opposites, they produce the same result. In the case of humanity, like individual earthlings, this scale moves in a spiral. It grows slowly to a point when suddenly leaps into the breaking point of the opposite side and slowly quietens down to near stillness and then starts growing again. Whenever humanity arrives at that particular point, energy and knowledge injection comes from the macrocosm to help wake us up and push earthling towards recovery. The interference opens our memory and starts seeking answers to questions. This urge sets up a new path for the enlightened few with spiritual awareness, and with hard work, these earthlings would pull the rest of humanity towards the Light. Sacred places built by the macrocosm are frequented by many to help see and know. These places I call the *fingerprints of the Gods.*

Without remembering the Great Work, humanity would be wasted.

If there is an above there has to be a below. In the case of earthlings below is under the ground. There are many underground civilizations who work for, or against us. How did they get there is a different story. I only want to mention the helping hand from those groups. The most visible result of their work are the crop-circles. They arrive at the very time of need with a prediction and teaching. Humanity as a whole doesn't know what to do with these beautiful formations. Somehow, I feel it is all for the better because we tend to destroy everything we do not understand and our comprehension is very limited.

4. Physical and Mental Evolution and the Purpose of Life – the Great Work

The Great Work, some people refer to it as Magnum Opus, is the interrelation of wholistic energies according to which the universe was and is created. Others might talk about it as the work of God however I want to avoid any misleading preconceptions here. It is usually taken for religious behaviour if one talks about God. It is especially true with Christianity. They tend to reduce God, the first knowledge that was able to multiply by division, to a human-like person who keeps you on a leash and only rewards you if you are fearful of his decisions. Since he is human-like he frequently changes his mind about rules and regulations and favours certain people more than others.

I could talk about the Great Work for weeks. However, this book is dedicated to the general outlook of events. Therefore, I give you those laws and regulations I feel fit. There is a basic structure to a happy existence that one needs to follow:

1. All Earthlings are equal – not the same –, they all should be granted the equal opportunity to evolve and deserve respect from others for they live in interrelation, and not respecting others comes down to the lack of respect towards the Self.

2. All creatures are responsible for their thoughts, words, and deeds, and also those of others. They should be conscious all the time and devote 100% of their attention to anything they are currently doing.

3. They should understand the creative power of thoughts. Words should be followed by action all the time.

4. Build a deep connection with the Creator force through

understanding the Self.

5. No person should be judged, for everyone gives 100% of one's abilities at every given moment.

6. Stay within the cycle of nature by following the macrocosmic ideas and deny the opportunities from the ego.

7. Take on the Initiations of the 4 elements to further the understanding of the Whole.

8. You should not be taken off the road by promises from the direction of easy paths. A Saint works on his own soul and his own spiritual evolution according to rules created by fellow human beings in the name of God. This action leads the way out of the cycle of nature.
A spiritually evolved person understands that one can only find happiness through experience and remaining an active segment of the universe.

9. Experiences should not be denied but work through them for they are the only way towards evolution. There are no problems in life, only unfinished or unsolved tasks.

I would like to give you the words of Hermes Trismegistos, translated by the editors of the Shire of Wisdom, here:

"If then you do not make yourself equal to God, you cannot apprehend God, for like is known by like. Leap clear of all that is corporeal, and make yourself grow to a like expanse with that greatness which is beyond all measure; rise up above all time and become eternal; then you will apprehend God. Think that for you nothing is impossible; deem that you are too immortal, and that you are able to grasp all things in your thought, to know every craft and every science; find yourself home in the haunts of every living creature; make yourself higher than all heights and lower than all depths; bring together in yourself all opposites of quality: heat and cold, dryness and fluidity; think that you are everywhere at once, on land and at sea, in heaven; thing that you are not yet begotten, that you are in the womb, that you are young, that you are old, that you have died, they you are in the world beyond the grave; grasp in your thoughts all this at once, all times and places, all substances and qualities and magnitudes together; then you can apprehend God. But if you shut up your soul in your body, and abase yourself, and say: "I know nothing, I can do nothing, I am afraid of earth and sea, I cannot mount to heaven; I do not know what I was, nor what I shall be", then what have you to do with God? For it is the height of Evil not to know God. But to be capable of knowing God, and to wish and hope to know It, is the road which leads straight to the Good..."

10. Everybody and everything carry opposites within, for they do not exist without one another. Stay on the bright side of the road but do not refuse to understand the dark.

I want to remind you here that there is only one life. To divide it into earthly and macrocosmic, material and spiritual is a great mistake for being spiritually aware should help your everyday life rather than take time and effort away from it.

5. Pyramid Forms in the Universe

With the introduction of the Uranus energies about 90 odd years back, earthlings' fascination with pyramids as forms suddenly jumped from almost non-existent to prominent. This fascination has resulted in a flood of published and unrecognized articles centred on the 2 most important pyramid structures: the complex on Giza plateau and the great pyramid of Chichen Itza. Speculations about their origin, age and purpose, like mushrooms that sprang from the ground, are either serve as entertainment or provide a train of thought to actually exercise the brain. I have met many suggestions however very few that excite me. There are 2 general categories with a slightly different viewpoint how these pyramids are approached. One would follow long-established factors about the planet and the other would try to find some interrelation between events. Although the latter is more interesting however, the lack of information would not provide fertile ground for comparison.

As everything, the attraction of the pyramids is the result of the shift in energies from Neptune to Uranus which allowed the subconscious to take part in existence and changed from the Neptune-Pisces symbol of the perfect square to the perfect triangle that is the symbol of Uranus.

We have talked about the 2 triangles slipping into each other as the symbol of the macro- and microcosmic interrelation and meeting of the 4 elements one of which, Fire comes from the macrocosm. In the space, the 2 triangles become 2 pyramids, actually 2 perfect pyramids.

The perfect pyramid is the smallest segment of life forms that moves on a spiral.

Going back to the pyramids of Giza, they are actually not perfect forms however the twist in them provides the secret I am going to talk about in my next book. On the top of each pyramid, there was a perfect crystal pyramid that actually served as an energy manipulator and star gateway between the 2 planes.

The pyramid complex of Giza was built at the very beginning of the 1st Sun Age by macrocosmic forces. It is a reminder of the Orion, the centre of the galaxy carrying its measurements. The seven pyramids complex – now only 3 is intact – marks the very centre of the equilateral triangle Earth's dry lands fit into when pushed together. Remarkably the complex is built in the vicinity of the Nile, the mirror of the Milky Way. Looking at the complex from above it is a descaled copy of the Orion and Milky Way at the time of Leo. The Sphinx itself faced Leo in the sky in this 2160-years period. We should not forget about the river delta as the Sex chakra of the planet.

Another important landmark is the step pyramid of Saqqara that was built even earlier than its counterpart in Giza. Although it is usually referred to as having 6 steps, however data recollecting the Exam of Knowledge that took part on the steps of the Saqqara pyramid, talks about 7 levels. Philosophers, physicists, mathematicians and astrologers gathered there once a year to weigh their knowledge on the famous step pyramid. After each successful level, the candidate was allowed to take the next step on it. An unsuccessful answer would result in failure and a jump from the height where the candidate finished the test.

The other important pyramid on earth is the step pyramid of Chichen Itza where the whole calendar and Sun Ages are built into the steps as reminders of the past and as an aid for the future. With the pyramids, there is another very important form and that is the obelisk. On top of each obelisk, there was a perfect pyramid. Later, they have been redesigned and rebuilt however they originally served as matrix catchers and energy boosters. There is an obelisk in every ancient Egyptian temple placed there with the utmost accuracy to do the work it is assigned to do. Today there are many obelisks as part of city planning and decoration.

Various healing methods work with energy manipulation. Although everything we do, eat, say or think, change the energies around, these methods put direct emphasis on certain points in the body or mind. The most known is acupuncture where cleansing the meridians, the flow of the energy is accomplished. Other methods, like REIKI, channel the energy and shift it into the ailing part of the body. In AKIA – the healing method is part of the philosophy – we use the obelisks within the body to rejuvenate and reorganize the 4 elements within. The physical body of an earthling has 33 obelisks. The places where they are as follows:

1 on the forehead
2 at the eyes
2 at the nose
2 ears
2 in the mouth
2 at the shoulders

2 upper arms

2 elbow

2 lower arms

2 wrists

2 palms

2 hips

2 thighs

2 knees

2 legs

2 ankles

2 feet

By activating the obelisks, the soul links up with the Syon centre on Orion 15, to enhance its frequency and become more adept to the quantum leap. This exercise and method should only be practiced by highly skilful AKIA healers, for the method carry extreme danger also.

There is Stonehenge which is claimed by different tribes and belief systems nevertheless, it was put on Earth prior to descend as a calendar and a reminder of the macrocosmic existence.

Drawings like in Peru and Great Britain carry symbols to trigger the subconscious and make us remember the time of the beginning.

Have you ever thought about how the numbers were created? Why do we have 10 of them? Well, because 10 is 9 + 1. And 9 is 3 x 3. Three is the representation of the equilateral triangle, the two opposite poles of the universe and everything in it, and nine is the mould of the two. On Earth, these 3 are the man, the woman and the child as Earth, Water and Air. The Holy Trinity of the interrelation between the two opposites blended into wholeness. It is the perfect side of a pyramid and the 3 earthly elements we need to master here in Earth School. Do not mistake it for the Christian Holy Trinity! In that conveniently everybody is a male.

The number 1 is the first. The First Knowledge that was able to multiply by division: The Creator of the universe.

The 10 numbers also represent the 10 perfect vowels. As numbers, to the universe vowels are the souls of words for without them communication would not exist. In early writings, only consonants were used to guard the Knowledge and the secret essence of the thought. It was the protection of the Great Work, for only those with adequate wisdom could read and understand the message. They were aware of the fact that important things are only visible for the *chosen individuals.* We still find this phenomenon in a few living languages.

The numbers

"1"

It is the highest form of existence

It depicts the Creator, the first knowledge that could multiply by division

It is the beginning of something new

It is in every number, in every body and in every thing

It is the smallest and the largest one-ness

There is no higher knowledge for human beings to understand

Its **symbol is the dot** that projected itself out to become a line.

"2"

The symbol of the 2 poles

The good and the bad

Creator and Humanity

Micro and Macrocosm

Every philosophy and religions come from it

Its **symbol is the straight line**

"3"

Is the number of Akasha

The fate

The karma

The past, present and future

The equilibrium between the 2 poles

The innocent child who is yet genderless

It is the number of life and death

It is the knowledge of the whole

Its **symbol is the equilateral triangle**

„4"

It is 3 + 1

The 4 basic elements

The 4 directions

The 4 basic characteristics of the Creator:

>Wisdom
>
>Love
>
>Almightiness
>
>Immortality

It means the total consciousness

It is the 4 pillars of the universe meaning

>Law, Order, Truth and Fulfilment

Its **symbol is the perfect square**

„5"

It is the image of the universe

It is the number 4 within the human being

It is half of the whole as the earthling is the half of whole, until develop himself into a one-ness.

It is the channel between Earth and the universe

Its **symbol is the 5 pointed** star

„6"

It is the opposite of 5.

The macrocosm

It points to the light where we can meet with the creator

It is the symbol of the magi

Its **symbol is the 6 pointed** star

„7"

It is the number of prosperity, productivity and fruitfulness

It is love in every form

The symbol of unity

Its **symbol is the 7 pointed equilateral** star

Meaning the 3 poles of humanity and 4 points of the Creator

„8"

It is the intellect of the human being

The knowledge and the mind

It is the number of magickal wisdom

Its **symbol is the equilateral 8 pointed star**, the four-dimensional form of the human being

„9"

It is the symbol of the astral world and depicts the First knowledge

It represents all the natural and astral magick and rituals

The sum of the true numbers are 9

$1+2+3+4+5+6+7+8+9=45=9$

Its **symbol is the 3 equilateral triangles**

„10"

It is the higher version of number 1

The commitment and fulfilment

The matter - for it is 2 digits

The symbol of the alchemists

It is 2 x 5

It depicts a leaped new beginning and endless possibilities as **"0"**

Its symbol is the circle with an 8 pointed cross

The letters

Every letter is a thought form, a principle. The shape of the figure carries data about its origin and of the person writing it. It really is a great shame that we use uniformed letters today. The root of the matter and the past disappeared; it lost its individuality.

The letters fill the universe with their vibrations even in written form. They are energies and should be pronounced on certain notes associated with individual letters. They also carry colours both of which we use for healing.

When the sound of a letter is formed the whole existence should be used. Take a breath through the Crown chakra, bring it down to the Base, hook the sound on it and release it to the universe. Therefore, it is important to consider the words we utter for they are energies and altering the surrounding by blending into it.

Every letter, like everything in the universe, has a number assigned to it according to the quality of its energy.

Earthlings need to learn to speak the Universal language of responsibility and consideration.

7. DNA, the Spiral of Life through the Tarot Deck

The tarot deck is the most popular fortune-telling tool in the Northern Hemisphere.

I use and teach various fortune-telling and reading techniques. I usually invent a new way every time when I am not satisfied with my students' intuition. And that is quite often. I will explain a few reading methods here.

Ribbon reading

Select 12 or 9 different coloured ribbons and cut them to a foot in length. A foot is 30.48 cm. As you can see, numbers are very important in my work, therefore I always follow the numbers related to Earth and connected to the universe. I also use measurements of the same quality.

Take your fortune-telling table cover and spread the ribbons out as shown above. You read the answers from the ribbon selected by the enquirer.

Paper reading

Take a piece of A4-size white paper. Ask the enquirer to think about the question and crease the paper while doing it. Read the forms and signs.

Coffee grout

I think you are familiar with this type of reading. It is done with Arabic, Turkish and Greek coffee when you drink it and leave the fine grout in the bottom of the cup. This technique is related to the Middle East.

Buzios

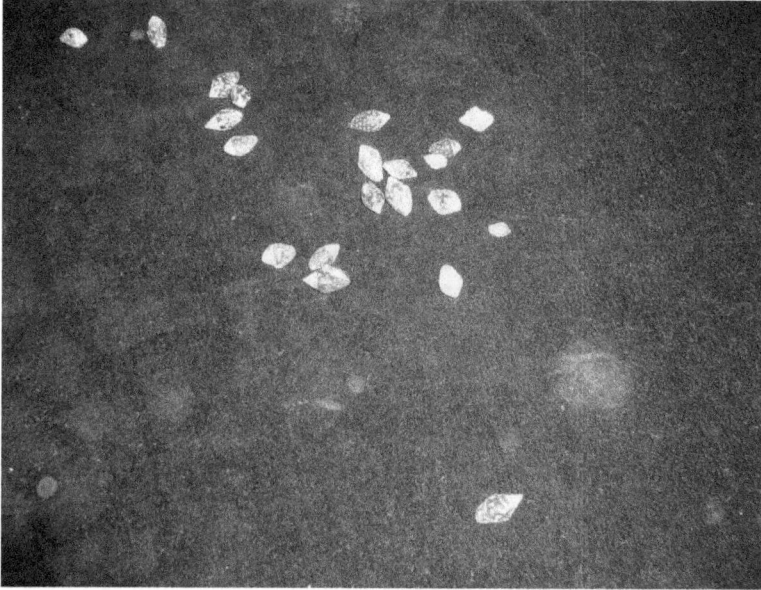

They are shells of sea creatures. I learned to read buzios in Brazil from the Orisha shaman people. It is great fun!

Energy reading

You look at the enquirer as an energy mass and the past, present and future open up for you. One needs a lot of information about energies and sharp intuition to do this form of reading.

Gypsy cards

There are various packs to use. Out of the several I have, I favour the Hungarian Gypsy pack. It has 36 cards, just the right amount, and the pictures are simple and understandable. These cards are used for earthly and everyday matters.

Tarot reading

We have arrived at my very favourite fortune-telling technique, the traditional tarot deck.

I do understand that there are many newly-created tarot packs are available. However, only the traditional tarot deck of 78 cards carries The Knowledge, the essence of the Macro and Microcosm and The Genesis of Humanity. I know these words sound pretty majestic, and one might not see their connection to the tarot nevertheless, I will do everything I can, to unveil the mystery behind the 78 cards.

First, we need to address those majestic words.

- ## The Knowledge

It is the understanding of interrelations in every aspect and every form of life in the universe. In other word, it is the information one is able to put into practice.

- ## Macrocosm and Microcosm

We earthlings have our own *cosmoses*. The microcosm is the place that one understands. The understanding might not be conscious, for comprehending a segment doesn't necessarily carry the knowing of the whole. However, it is the place one feels comfortable and confident in. For some people, the microcosm ends at the front door of the house, and for others, it stretches over galaxies. The rest of the endless universe is the macrocosm. In one word we can say that macrocosm is everybody's strange and unknown place.

- ## The Genesis of Humanity

It is the *time*, the *how*, the *from where* and the *where to* of the beginning.

Through the deck, you can also learn to understand yourself. It is a mirror of your thoughts, deeds and words; the fore-mentioned micro and macrocosm. It is a mirror for the universe. For me a traditional tarot deck - that is of 78 cards - is an organic

energy; more specifically, an earthling. It senses organic
energies and changes accordingly.

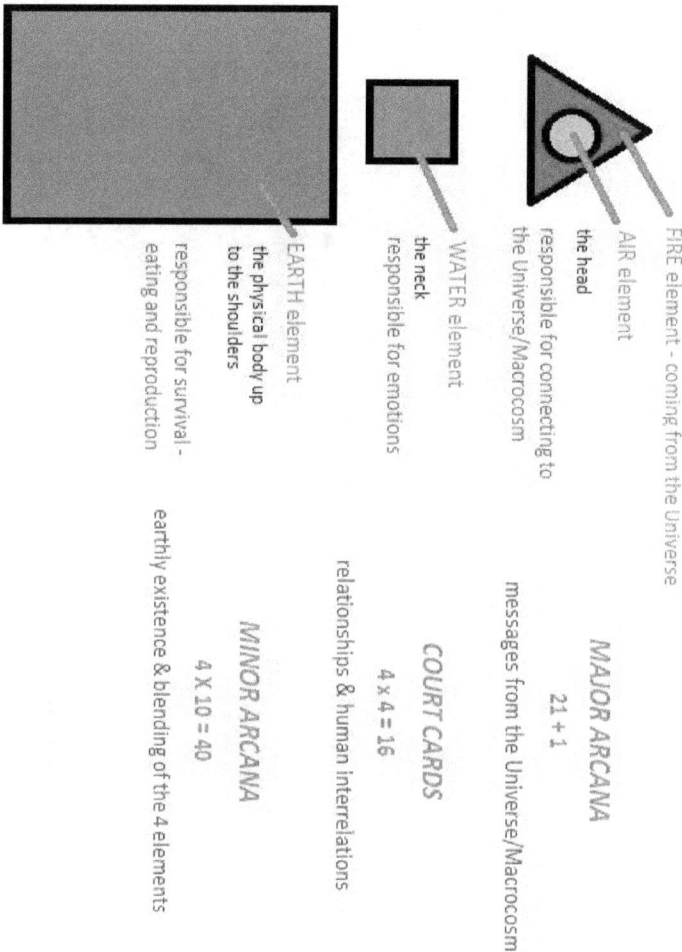

FIRE element - coming from the Universe

AIR element
the head
responsible for connecting to
the Universe/Macrocosm

WATER element
the neck
responsible for emotions

EARTH element
the physical body up
to the shoulders
responsible for survival -
eating and reproduction

MAJOR ARCANA
21 + 1
messages from the Universe/Macrocosm

COURT CARDS
4 x 4 = 16
relationships & human interrelations

MINOR ARCANA
4 X 10 = 40
earthly existence & blending of the 4 elements

The tarot deck is made up of 3 parts, alike a human being. They are the lower body, the neck and the head; the Minor Arcana, Court cards and the Major Arcana respectively.

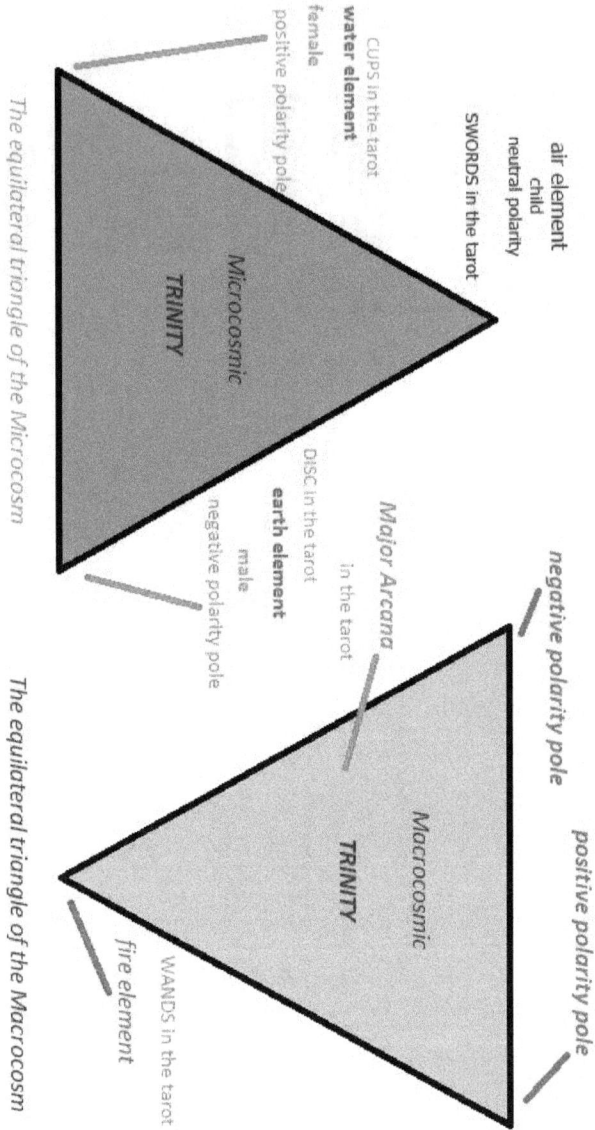

The equilateral triangle of the Microcosm

SWORDS in the tarot
air element
child
neutral polarity

CUPS in the tarot
water element
female
positive polarity pole

Microcosmic
TRINITY

DISC in the tarot
earth element
male
negative polarity pole

Major Arcana
in the tarot

The equilateral triangle of the Macrocosm

Macrocosmic
TRINITY

negative polarity pole

positive polarity pole

WANDS in the tarot
fire element

The 3 represents the Trinity of the 2 poles and the perfect blend. It also represents the 3 elements we are to master here on Earth. These are the Earth, the Water and the Air. Earth is the male, as he is more attached to the ground; Water is the female, for she is more emotional, and the child is the Air because through its innocence and openness it is the nearest to the Creator force. The child is the upright peak of the microcosmic equilateral triangle.

The first part of the tarot deck, the **Minor Arcana**, mirrors everyday earth connected living. These are the 4 element cards of 4 x 10. Apart from the 3 elements mentioned we are fortunate enough to receive fire from the macrocosm, to widen our horizon, to push us towards experiences and to lend us power, strength and courage. In another word, Earth element - the physical identity - is represented by the discs; Water elements - the emotional identity - is by the cups; Air element - the spiritual identity - is by the swords and Fire element - the mystical identity - is by the wands.

Thinking about it a bit deeper, this group is 3 + 1 for Fire comes from above; reassuring us that we are not alone, for the Creator force is blending into our Trinity or perfect triangle depicting our life. It also serves as the symbol of Uranus to further the knowledge of Neptune and conveniently make up the sides of the pyramid. The 4 also stands for the four phases of the Moon cycle.

The symbol of **Neptune** earlier of **Pisces** also

Represents the 4 elements, the 4 directions, the moon cycles etc...

It is the base of the pyramid

The 3 + 1

Represents the interrelations of the whole existence.

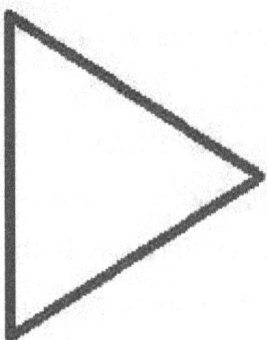

The symbol of Uranus.

It is the side of the pyramid.

The perfect 3

The 10 naturally represents the ten perfect numbers with their effective nature and the ten planets of the solar system.

$$10 = 3 \times 3 + 1.$$

Here the 1 is the ace, depicting the equal possibilities we all have. Not in the everyday sense though. We have equal opportunities to lose karma, fulfil the contracts, experience, feel and grow.

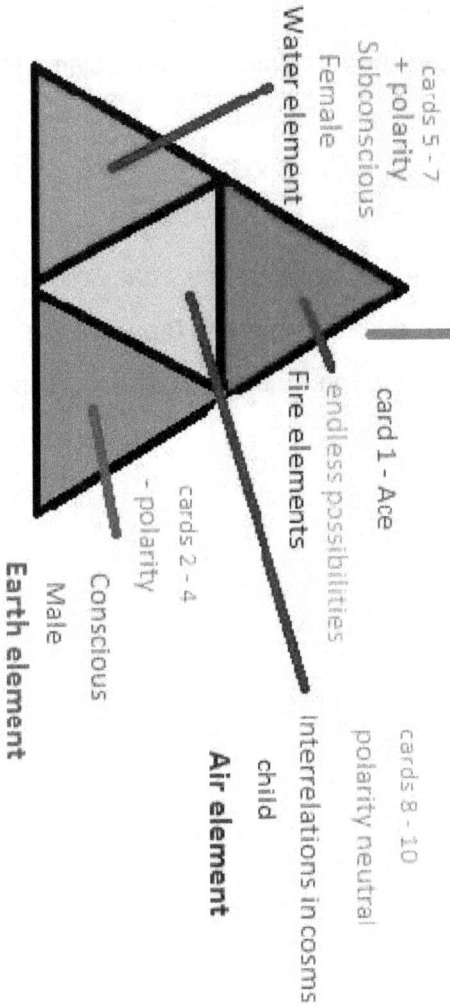

The perfect triangle as the essence of the Universe

cards 5 - 7
+ polarity
Subconscious
Female
Water element

card 1 - Ace

endless possibilities

Fire elements

cards 8 - 10
polarity neutral

Interrelations in cosms
child
Air element

cards 2 - 4
- polarity
Conscious
Male
Earth element

Within the 10 there are 3 groups of 3, again depicting the 3 elements. The number 1 is the ace with the power and opportunities. The numbers between 2 and 4 are Earth energies, the numbers from 5 to 7 are Water, and from 8 to 10 are Air within each element. The higher the number, the more experience it shows. Experience is not equal to physical wealth or wisdom. Sometimes we need to run a few circles before realizing the moral of the story. However, it presents the possibility of growing. Each group of 3 cards shows a circle in a spiral as it reaches for the macrocosmic energy.

The 3 piles also represent the 3 lower energy centres. Pile 1 would speak for Earth and corresponds with the **Base chakra**, pile 2 would be Water and corresponds with the **Sex chakra,** and pile 3 would be Air and corresponds with the **Solar Plexus**. It is the most complicated group of the deck. It mirrors the everyday existence, works with the elements and their effects on the physical body. The mirroring result of this group would show on the lower part of the body, from shoulders downwards. The next group is the 4 x 4 Court cards. They depict your different relationships and emotional existence within them. Again, we see the number 4 that is the four elements, the four directions, the four cycles of the Moon and Sun, the four basic Universal Rules of Truth, Order, Law and Fulfilment. It is the four sides of the pyramid and the perfect square that is the symbol of Pisces and Neptune. Emotions are higher than basic earthy fulfilments.

Taking parts in relationships shows a growing procedure, when one is not completely tied to Earth and has the courage to get into unprecedented situations. In this pile, each card depicts a circle on the spiral, as they represent the journey through the 4 elements within each. On the physical body, the result of the emotional happenings show on the neck, that is the throat, the mouth and the teeth. Very often spreads into the digestive system for digestion starts in the mouth. The 4 circle represents the 4 upper energy centres. These are the **Heart chakra,** the **Throat chakra,** the **Forehead chakra** and the **Crown chakra.**

Now we arrived at the 22 cards of the Major Arcana. They represent Fate and Universal involvement. The number 22 stands for the twenty-two star-formations of the currently reigning zodiac, carrying its essence; the twenty-two consonants, the number 4 with all its qualities, the 3 + 1 for these cards are in reality 21 + 1 with the Fool taking 0.

As you can see from the numbers, the Major Arcana carries the essence of all the other cards in the pack.

The Fool is the Creator force with its endless possibilities, choices, experiences and wisdom. It is everything. It is the whole universe, the Great Cycle by itself.

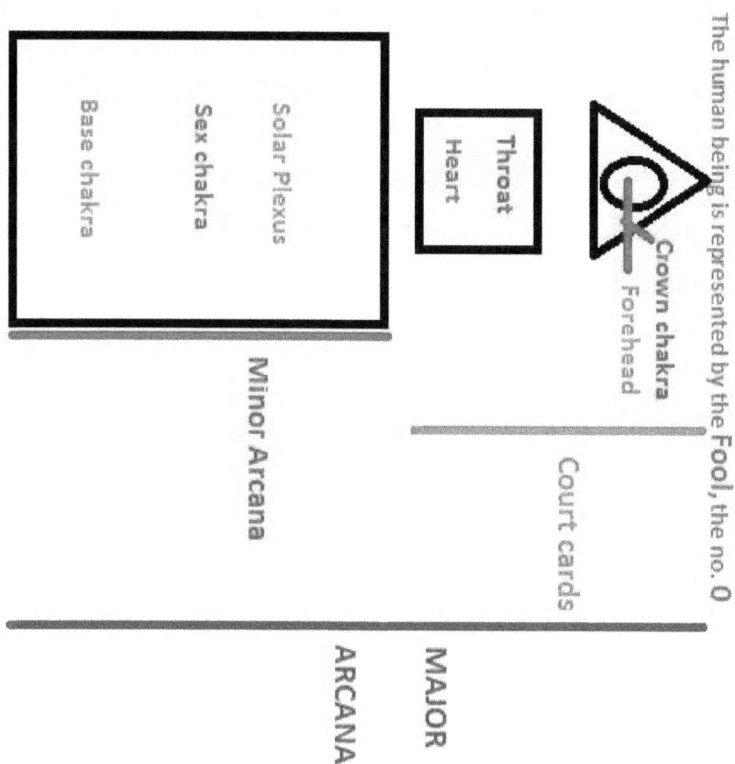

The human being is represented by the Fool, the no. 0

Crown chakra
Forehead

Throat
Heart

Solar Plexus
Sex chakra
Base chakra

Minor Arcana

Court cards

MAJOR
ARCANA

Looking at the rest of the cards, they make up 7 piles; 7 circles of the spiral. They deal with all the 7 energy centres, the 3 + 4. Apart from its basic quality, number 7 depicts the 2 equilateral triangles slipped into each other and creating a Great Oneness. They are also the cycles of the Moon.

Each card in the Major Arcana stands for an experience one needs to go through to arrive at the true fulfilment of the path, however, they all carry the essence of the universe within. They are the pulling power, the cautions and path-finders. They are the human life that starts with the Magician and ends with the universe. The 7 circles together make up a greater circle of the spiral. The cycle when you are not afraid to pay attention to the universe, the macrocosm; when you are not afraid to experience the unknown.

It is the fulfilment of living.

4th Secret: Truth Behind Popular Expressions

1. Love

It is definitely the most talked about and the most sought after feeling amongst earthlings. Countless meanings were given to the word, which were formed and altered according to moral understandings. Since the beginning of the 5th Sun Age around b.c.e. 3.113 religions started to form groups around their limited understanding of the world to give hope to the survivors of the disasters hitting the planet at the end of the 4th Sun Age. I only mention this event because religions play a very strong role in our emotional state and as such in our view towards love.

Regardless of its aim this word will always be connected to sexuality and feelings related to it. This is the reason behind the mystery and misunderstandings surrounding this expression. To eliminate the pain certain explanations are added like motherly love, fatherly love, friendly love, romantic love, sexual love etc. These expressions are to certify the responsibility attached. However, these explanations do not clear up the situation at all, for even earthlings belonging to the same religious or social group with some sort of global understanding would look at the word with their own individual thoughts in mind.

Let us look at motherly love as an example. It has been drastically altered by the brainwashing machinery and insecurity produced by society. Mothers tend to spoil and cling to their children now more than ever. They allow themselves to be enslaved by the offspring by doing basic chores, taking every responsibility away from the child by solving connected issues and make important decisions on their behalf regardless of the consequences and future effects on their lives. Others stay away and presumably give the young ones the freedom of development without guidance.

Looking at any kind of relationship we are mainly interested in the related feelings of the other person or persons concerned and we interpret them according to our viewpoint. The truth as always will be the result of one's relation to the given situation. There is a love most people think to be the purest and it is the love of God. However, if you look at it a bit closer, you'll realize that different religions and individuals within the group, look at this love conveniently altered to their own personal preference. In the end, this God becomes very much like a human being. He – as it is usually referred to – is very selective when it comes to spreading love. He is only available to those belonging to the same belief - system group. He definitely favours appreciation, especially material, and demands all sorts of sacrifices in return for some of his love. There is a mad race to fulfil his manmade requirements and receive a morsel of his abundance. It is the best example of earthling falling into their own trap.

Concluding my little essay, I would add that God, or as I call it, the Creator as the first Knowledge, able to multiply by division, is neutral. So is Love. No requirements, no conditions attached only pure interrelated energies, acceptance, helping and caring.

2. Empathy

In our fast-changing, always challenging and sometimes overwhelmingly difficult life we learn to appreciate if someone connects to our feelings; especially when they are the result of some sort of suffering. We also tend to like people with empathic abilities.

There are many questions that come to my mind regarding the subject. I would give you the answers without the questions.

Empathy usually needs 2 participants. There is one, who suffers and the other one, who takes the feeling on board without any particular reason. However, either groups or individuals, the partakers have something similar regarding the event that triggered the feeling. Since related energies like each other it becomes very obvious that they also have an alike understanding of the particular matter. This understanding derives from the social background, upbringing, belief systems and spiritual comprehension of life. It means that if a friend complains about her husband cheating on her one would develop empathy only if one is convinced that it is unacceptable. One might also feel connected if one has already experienced it at one stage, and I still carry the hurt within.

There are people, who would take on the feeling in the extent of developing the particular illness related to the other person. If let's say your digestive system is suffering and you have a constant stomach ache as the result of some emotional upheaval the empathic person would have the same illness even if there seems to be no trauma behind the scene in his or her life. It actually happens because this person has an inclination towards not only the suffering part but the particular thought-form that caused it. Putting it into an example the digestive system physically suffers as the result of chewing on thoughts that bother us without being able to release them. The reason behind it is fear. Fear from the future, the past, the present, people around, the family the religion. Let us stay with the example I used earlier. You think that your husband is cheating on you. You will nurture the thought for a while for you are afraid to face the situation and come out and ask him. First of all, you wouldn't think that he was going to tell you the truth. With this idea, you have already planted the strongest seed for suffering for whatever he says you won't believe, and at this point your partnership is over; unless you change your mind and carry on loving him unconditionally.

Taking the first approach on board, you would waste a lot of time on seeking others with similar experience or those who would show empathy. It is needed to reassure you that you are not alone with your problem and also you would be able to come out and say that you are a victim. This way you can all suffer together strengthening the feeling in each other by belonging to the group of *good* people who are taken advantage of by the *bad* ones.

The theory of the sufferers being good comes from the modern Christians or I would say from the New Testament where everybody who suffers is called good or saint. We use the term yes, *she is a saint she suffered enough* quite loosely in our everyday living without actually giving it a thought. Suffering is a choice. However, it might come from the misconception that life on Earth is suffering and those who suffer go to Heaven.

Although we are here to learn that we do through experience and it might take us into the state of momentary suffering, however, every experience should end with a closure rather than preventing us to get into new tasks of learning.

There is another type of empathy towards those we consider less fortunate than us because of mental or physical handicap and other suffering related events. Spiritually speaking their lives is the result of choices the soul made before coming down to Earth in order to help with learning, experiencing and evolving.

As a healer, I often develop momentary empathy towards my patients to help understand the task ahead of me. However, as the most important part of my work I would urge them to assess the past take an inventory of it and look forward to life without the burdens of the past.

Strangely enough, we do not seem to take on joy or happiness from others. As if we were a bit ashamed of being happy. Can you imagine creating HAPPY groups and through Empathy we would spread the word of JOY, HEALTH and HAPINESS.

Well, when you are ready you can knock on my door.

3. Belief

It is one of those words that we interpret very loosely nowadays. We use it when we are not certain of something and also when we are very sure of our truth. When we trust something to happen the way we desire and when there are doubts in our mind. The most common way of using this word is concerning our religious stand.

In Europe, it is almost none-acceptable not to belong to some sort of religious group as if it was the basic requirement of living. On the surface, we like to favour Far-Eastern religions we spice with Christianity even Wicca that is already an altered version of the Art of Witchcraft however, Christianity is the one that shapes our way of living and way of thinking. Not really because we believe in it. Although, almost everybody goes through a Christening ceremony at a tender age, it is done as a custom rather than conviction. We do not really think much about this custom however, it has a karmic effect that actually help shape our way of thinking. As everything with human beings, this belief system is on the surface. When questioned, members of this particular faith would say they believe in the Bible. They do not really say they believe in the Ten Commandments, although it is the base of Christian faith but they press their beliefs in the Book and the prophet Jesus. It is all very well, for religious belief is private however, it is more and more common to state the Christian prophet as The Prophet and furthermore, as God, the Creator. As if nothing existed before or beside. I am not here now to talk about Christianity but unfortunately, I cannot avoid the subject while talking about beliefs. I find it is the core of many beliefs in life. I am certain, we agree upon the fact that the belief in the mythology of Christianity comes from fear and as such it is the result of insecurity, lack of knowledge and understanding. In the 21st century C.E. (common era) when we use the phrase *seeing is believing* we readily give into the unknown when our belief system is concerned. It is like shifting responsibility and allowing ourselves to blame the system or someone else for the misfortune and unhappiness of life. This belief system is very dangerous indeed. Since we give into unknown powers we give away the driving seat and with it the responsibility of our deeds and thoughts. As a result, we become lost in life that generates unhappiness and sorrow. On the other hand, we are taught to believe that suffering makes us a better person. In many ways it is true if it is the result of experiencing something new and we learn from it. Self-inflicted suffering is idle, and might give us a prominent place in heaven as we tempt to believe. However, it alters the purpose of life and make Earth an unhappy place to be. This belief system makes us intolerant and suspicious towards those with different beliefs. Mostly because we do not understand them, and we don't make an effort to do so.

The insecurity we gain from religious beliefs would lead us to become part of the global mass consciousness when we follow ideas without questioning them. We believe that they are the followers of the truth. Yes, but what is truth? And whose truth is truer?

Truth is an illusion for it is different for everybody. It is the straight result of our intelligence, experience and belief system. Bearing it in mind that we do not actually see what is really there for the eye initially absorbs the rays of light reflected back from the object or subject and send an impulse to the conscious and the subconscious; at the same time waiting for their agreement to create a picture you would consider the Truth.

We also need to touch upon the subject of spirituality. It is again a belief that spirituality comes with religion and embrace. I would like to shed some light on the fundamental difference between the two.

A religion is a set of beliefs and practices centred upon specific supernatural and moral claims about reality and often codified, while spirituality is a path to reach and become one with the Creator Force. In one word, religion talks about what you cannot ever achieve and spirituality shows you the way to arrive there.

I believe that one's belief system is changeable by experience, knowledge, openness and tolerance. I believe that creating our own consciousness would raise the quality of life and we could look upon Earth as the Heaven of life.

4. Goodness

The basic understanding of the word varies according to the social background, religious belief, education and upbringing of the individual or group of people it is related to.

The word itself derives from God who is supposed to be always good and kind. Looking at the supernatural being watching us from above, dressed in a long white robe with a constant smile on his old and weary face that framed with a substantial white beard, the *Good God* is always there to keep us on the right track, scolds us – never punishes – when we forget about his rules and regulations and gives us a hand when we fall. This behaviour pattern would definitely match up to Godness or goodness in most of our minds.

Following this train of thoughts, I arrived at the conclusion that goodness is above us and it has nothing to do with human beings. It is a behaviour pattern of a man-created myth that is beyond reach therefore it gives us the green light not to follow suit.

When we talk about something being good, it turns out to be pleasing and enjoyable. The goodness of an earthling could be the general view of a person, who seemingly lives up to the expectation of those in the community. These anticipations do not go deep, only brushing the surface for 2 apparent reasons: the first is to establish the view of the community as a path to acceptance and becoming a member of the herd. The second is based upon the preconception that if one is a member of a certain community, he or she can be judged by the behaviour pattern of the community, and instantly considered to be a good person. Then again, if you look into the so-called good communities they are usually established in areas of comfort, security and wealth, oozing the idea that good people are bound to have a certain background of material wealth. One can actually turn this view around and say that the Good God gave earthlings wealth as a reward for being good. Whatever the direction is material seems to be a decisive factor of goodness. I know of communities, even countries where it is an established part of the basic understanding that poor countries are left behind when God was giving wealth away as a prize for goodness. Well, if God is so pretentious then we have the clear license to be. However, do not forget that this God was created by people who are mirroring their behaviour pattern on the Almighty. It is sort of funny, isn't it? The story of He creating us amongst everything is just a comfortable twist.

There are also certain preconceptions with professions like doctors, teachers, judges, police, nurses, nuns and members of the clergy ... etc. that benefit from instant respect and goodness would be associated with their lives.

What is goodness then? Generally speaking, it is an act of understanding. An unconditional, therefore non-judgemental view of events and people; where everything and everybody is given an equal chance to grow and succeed on the spiritual plane. It is an aid that points one in the right direction after being lost or taken off the track.

This is the only way how goodness works. Without this comprehension goodness doesn't exist for what is good for one it is definitely bad for someone else and lack of information brings hasty decisions in the meaning of the word.

5. Acceptance

Earthlings live according to many different belief systems and behaviour patterns most of which come from family teachings, religious beliefs and upbringing. The effects during the tender age of childhood carry more importance than the rest of life for they provide the foundation for the rules and regulations and basic morality of life, with the view about acceptance amongst them.

There are different levels of acceptance however there is one similarity: they are all decisions. Furthermore, they are verbal or written contracts between people.

Earthlings detest changes and as the consequence decision-making is not one of their forte. They linger upon situations asking everybody around in order to figure out the most favourable outcome of the big step. The worry doesn't come from the consequences on their personal life but from the impact the new step makes on the relationship they have with others. Here comes the *good person* syndrome when the world becomes the market place where caring and consideration are announced. This way the decision is made not entirely from your own heart but with help from others therefore you might think that the responsibility is also shared and the consequences would fall upon those concerned. Naturally, it is an illusion. Whatever happens, the responsibility for your own actions always comes down to you. It is eased by the blame you might consider putting on other people or the environment however the fact remains and it is the unavoidable consequences of the agreement you entered into. Acceptance is a direct involvement and connection to somebody else's existence while decision making usually affects the surroundings indirectly. Although the first is far more permanent than the latter, it is easier and sooner produced due to the misconception of the word. When we talk about acceptance, hardship and suffering appear in the mind, pleasure and happiness given up for the sake of granting them to somebody else as if these feelings were limited editions and one needed to queue up to take possession of them. This action is the play of the ego when we hope for a reward after suffering. It is an illusion. We are not here on Earth to suffer but learn.

There is no reward waiting for you after suffering for it is your choice and your decision to do so. Happiness and pleasure are abundantly available to everybody, who is ready to handle them. None of them come from the environment but dwell and grow within.

There is also another way of accepting. It comes from a deeper understanding of the universe. You accept that you are not in control therefore there are events you cannot change. This is the greatest acceptance and it opens the road to happiness and fulfilment.

Love is closely related to acceptance. Since love is neutral as the Creator force, it is also unconditional; meaning that you accept everything that loved ones do, without questioning their deeds. One should not accept a situation out of fear or false pretences. Suffering is a self-indulgent feeling that produces only slow and low-frequency energy adding to the problems of the world.

Acceptance should never bring unhappiness or sadness. It is a choice that permanently alters the lives of the people concerned. When you are able to accept this thought, then the road to happiness opens up for you.

6. Peace

In our everyday lives, we think of the word **peace** as the opposite of **war** and we usually place it on the physical plane.

If we want to understand peace, we need to look at war. Why do we have wars? The explanation we are given is that war is for survival. Needless to say, that it is a very naive approach, for wars on Earth do not fall into this category. Countries invading others and killing people justify their deeds and find excuses chiselled into the brain of all concerned by the mass media. The brainwashing machinery empties the mind and leaves it idle without questions and original opinions. Since we rely upon the media more and more, we are in the process of losing the power of thinking and moral understanding of the world. We become the media machinery itself. We might even think that we do it for peace. It is true; we are the part of the mass consciousness, whatever it stands for, to be left in peace in exchange for loyalty. No thoughts are wasted on looking behind the curtains and understanding effects and counter effects. While we turn our back on global issues the so-called civilized nations systematically demolish half of the world killing everything and everybody on the way. And we think that we are at peace.

Left in peace means that you are an individual who would rather pay attention to private needs, thoughts and regulations. It also means that you do not favour changes, traditions are important and a set behaviour pattern draws your path towards the aim of your life. In one word you are stubborn, narrow-minded and earthly. You do not understand the interrelation of energies and the fact that you are going to suffer from the events for which you are affected regardless.

Let us get back to war. As the Great Work faded into the background and Atlantis became a myth the insecurity of Earthlings grew. By the end of the 4th Sun Age around b.c.e. (before common era) 3.113 the understanding of earthly existence, the feeling of oneness and the ancient knowledge disappeared and religious mythology started to spread to give hope and security to earthlings. At the end of Taurus – Spring Venus era the first religion was established with its rules and set demands for redemption keeping the Golden Bull as the symbol of their teachings. Two thousand odd years later, at the end of the Aries-Mars and the beginning of the Pisces-Neptune era another one sprang from the ground with even more mythology to fill the gaps provided by the first one. Naturally, it took the Lamb and the Fish as symbols. By that time Earthlings lost the attachment to the universe and the confidence in their own values for these religions are set around a supernatural power dressed in human body as an example of the beyond reach. Later other philosophies were established as religions with a friendlier approach; however, insecurity and fear are always stronger and without tolerance towards changes therefore they are constantly attacked by the previous group.

Being an aggressor, the one who kills, shows the lack of peace and morality. I always wonder when countries spend a lot of money and time to devote to the so-called glorious past. I find it totally morbid to celebrate bullying and killing.

One could say that these facts are not important to peace. Well, one is mistaken, for peace derives from and dwells within. It is the result of your thoughts about the world, humanity and yourself. It is something either easy or very hard to achieve depending on your standing point. The wider your horizon is the closer you get to this indescribable feeling of fulfilment, tolerance and beauty. When you understand who you are, what are you doing here and the fact that everything is interrelated and that you are responsible for your deeds and thoughts. When you arrive at the point of loving everything and everybody around you unconditionally; when you realize that human beings are equal regardless of colour and social background; when you get curious enough to learn about the unknown rather than judging it without understanding; when you are brave enough to form your own opinion on matters then you can say that you are at peace.

Peace is not motionless at all. It is a conscious way of living and evolving.

7. Happiness

Happiness is the result of one's relationship with the universe. It is a philosophy, a point of view. Although we have this misconception that happiness depends on the state of the current companionship in life, it actually dwells within and mirrors the understanding of existence and the earthling's individual thought forms about the word. You might say that the same idea was mentioned before in this book related to other aspects of life. You are right for at the end of the road life results from one's understanding of the universe at a given time and aspect.

Staying with *happiness,* it is an overwhelming emotional state that occurs when the individual earthling reaches the point of fulfilment that brings clarity and understanding of the interrelations.

This procedure follows the idea of peace and harmony earthlings seek as the ultimate result of good living, not realizing that they entrap themselves in the greatest pitfall in existence that is stillness, no change therefore no motion.

As a cycle, life is a Catch 22 provided by the pushing – pulling motion of the conscious and the sub-conscious. It is the Ying and Yan motion. Although the soul is immortal the physical body has its time limits and as the result a cycle of earthly living is restricted to the well-functioning of this evolutionary tool. It is, for earthlings spend a lifetime to protect it by putting a roof over it, clothes, clean feed and comfort it. Take to the gym, put it through emotional effects and all kinds of pleasure. We do that because it is through the body we experience and evolve. This motion keeps the body alive.

On the other hand, in the mind we rush through life, only touching the steps we planned to walk while thinking about the next station on the row.

5th Secret: Exercises and Meditations for Everyday Use

1. Meeting your Guides

Guides are helpers from the higher plane. Their duty is to guide the soul of an earthling through the obstacles of being an earthling. Guides only work on the sixteen earth-like planets since they are not needed anywhere else.

The work of a guide used to start at the moment the soul gets into Shambala soon after leaving its physical body. As reincarnation stopped Shambala is packed with inexperienced souls wishing to come down here. That is the time when decisions are made. These decisions are very important from the point of the soul and the universe. The soul needs to find the adequate family into which it wishes to reincarnate, to further the education assign to each soul. Furthermore, the program has to be set.

Guides have real knowledge of past, present and future. They travel freely between dimensions and time zones. This ability gives them a fair advantage, however, can cause misunderstandings also. They need precise parameters when help is asked for. This data should be provided by the guided soul. It means that you must know your guides before real help can get to you. I use the word *knowing*, in the true sense which means meeting, talking to, listening to, communicating with, observing the main characteristics of ...and so on. A strong trust should be built between you and your guides, a two ways street with appreciation, respect and love.

During an Earth-life time a soul usually has more than one set of guides. Every time the soul manages to climb a step on the steep ladder of spiritual education a change of personal helpers takes place, a bit like in a school, where your educators vary according to your grades.

Sit down on the ground, with your back straightened and your legs crossed. Open your knees as much as you can; your arms comfortably beside you or on the knees. Relax.

Breathe slowly and deeply from above through the top of your head. Bring the air down along the spine. One-two-three-in and one-two-three-out. One-two-three-in and one-two-three-out.

After reaching steady and deep breathing, imagine that a golden light comes towards your Crown chakra on the top of your head. Let it in through the energy centre and bring it down to the Heart where this golden light makes its way into the universe forming a golden pathway, like a yellow brick road into the distance.

Now imagine that you become small, step out of your body and start walking the pathway. Observe as you walk. After a while, you reach a forest. There are all sorts of creatures there: animals, insects and vegetation. Do not be afraid, ask them questions if you wish and wait for the answers. Continue your journey through the forest until you find a meadow, full of different coloured flowers and butterflies. You'll find that they are also good for conversation. The Big Fireball is sending warmth and caresses you gently. The path leads to a wooden bridge that lies over a chatty creek. Look at your image in the water as you walk across. On the other side of the bridge, you catch sight of an abode of some kind. It can be anything.

You walk to the door and step in. Greet the two beings you find inside. They are your guides. Ask them who they are and the name they listen to and the way of connecting with them. If there is nobody yet do not despair but wait for your guides to come.

When the conversation is over, thank them nicely, say your farewells and close the door behind you. Walk through the bridge, look at your image in the water once again and continue the path across the meadow, back to the forest, all along to the heart chakra on the golden light. Step into yourself and become aware of your surrounding once again. Pull in the pathway, send it back to the universe with thanks and come back to your existence.

Sometimes a blockage of fear prevents you from seeing your guides therefore you might need to repeat the exercise.

2. Basic Cleansing and Healing

Sit down on the ground, with your back straightened and your legs crossed. Open your knees as much as you can; your arms comfortably beside you or on the knees. Relax.

Breathe slowly and deeply from above through the top of your head. Bring the air down along the spine. One-two-three-in and one-two-three-out. One-two-three-in and one-two-three-out.

Imagine that roots are coming out of the sole of your feet. They go under the ground into the soil. As you breathe in the dark earth energy comes up into your body more with every breath until it covers your hair and nails and you become this energy yourself.

Do not be afraid of the dark colour. It is only in the conditioned mind where dark depicts evil. The best and most fertile soil is black and now you can take advantage of its healing and cleansing power also.

As you are filled with earth energy feel its warmth and let it caress your body; bathe your ailing organs in it and let it collect all the residues left behind by food, thoughts, illnesses and events.

When finished with the healing imagine that a vast beam of golden light from the universe comes through your Crown. As you breathe in, come into your existence more and more, pushing out the dark earth energy that collected the residues and illnesses from your body, until the 2 energies blend in your aura and both become golden like the Sun.

Extend your aura with the light to 9 feet all around and invite the astral body of your loved ones into it for healing. When the enjoyment is over, send them all home; reduce your aura by letting the golden light out of it, release the light back to the universe with thanks.

This is a good morning meditation to start the day with.

3. Communicating with a Tree

Vegetation is the most intelligent organic energy on Earth. I know we like to think we are but generally, we are very far away from the basic understanding of existence. A vegetable lives in harmony with itself and with the universe while earthlings arrogantly deny this connection.

One day I sent my students up to visit an herb garden on Saturn when Geri came back with a fascinating message:

"A plant doesn't consider the rooting procedure work for it needs the roots for survival, and looks at it as an essential part of life."

Absolutely delightful! Everything we do we consider work and we moan about it. If we have a job we moan because we need to go there and do something; if we don't then it is the subject of suffering. We behave as if we are doing the universe a favour by merely existing.

Trees are the most intelligent of them all. They are connections between above and below. They carry information and data. As they interrelate all over the planet, a tree in Europe would hear the cries of cutting trees in the rainforest. They are able to forecast natural disasters, earthquakes and floods just as much as they can communicate with other planets.

If you wish to converse with a tree you need to befriend it prior to the event. They vibrate on a high frequency therefore you need to get used to each other and find the best way of performing the task. Follow your intuition on this procedure.

When the proper connection is established step to the tree and ask for a small twig.

Sit down on the ground, facing the tree on the Eastern side, with your back straightened and your legs crossed. Open your knees as much as you can; your arms comfortably beside you or on the knees. Relax.

Breathe slowly and deeply from above through the top of your head. Bring the air down along the spine. One-two-three-in and one-two-three-out. One-two-three-in and one-two-three-out.

Make yourself comfortable as if you were sitting inside the tree. Look at its charkas. Some would be under the ground so you need to look hard. Other times you find that you need to communicate through a leaf for it is the best place for connection at the given moment. When it is clear which of its chakra is used for communication let it build a connection with one of your energy centres.

Through your Crown chakra, let the highest frequency energy of the universe, the golden light in, and bring it down to the corresponding chakra through which you send the golden light over to the tree to get properly connected.

The next step is that you need to ask for a communication

symbol from the tree. It is a necessity for it interprets the languages used and helps to get into the awareness of the tree. To further the communication skills, imagine that you put the received symbol into your Solar Plexus and bring it up to the Heart where it strengthens.

A tree is able to bring answers to question about past, present and future events.

When the conversation finished you allow the symbol to travel back to your Solar Plexus, remove it and give it back to the tree. Pull back the golden light and through the Crown chakra send it back to the universe with thanks.

Send back the connection from the tree, thank it for the work and kindness and walk away.

Do every step of the closing exercise, for it can damage your energy field if it is left abandoned. Pay special attention to the symbols given.

4. Become a Flower

This is a very exciting and interesting exercise to understand the shift in awareness and to step out of the physical body.

Sit down on the ground, with your back straightened and your legs crossed. Open your knees as much as you can; your arms comfortably beside you or on the knees. Relax.

Breathe slowly and deeply from above through the top of your head. Bring the air down along the spine. One-two-three-in and one-two-three-out. One-two-three-in and one-two-three-out.

This meditation starts - as actually many - very similarly to the *yellow brick road* walk.

Through the forest you arrive to the meadow where there are beautiful wild flowers bathe in the sunshine. Look for a healthy one you like, greet it and find out if it was willing to work with you throughout this meditation. After a firm yes from the flower sit down on the ground facing it with your back to the East. Slow your breathing down to the usual rhythm. As you inhale slowly, you transfer your awareness into the flower. Do it with 17 breaths, being aware of the changes always. When you *become* the flower itself, keep all your senses open, take in the experience and store it in your mind to remember when the time comes.

Then shift your energy back to your physical body step by step, taking 17 breaths. Look at the flower again, see how it changed with your energy. Well, it might have withered; do not worry however, for it is going to survive the exercise.

Thank the flower for the gracious act, say your farewells and take the yellow brick road back to the Heart.

Finish as it is given in the first meditation.

5. Full Moon Exercise

Sit down on the ground, with your back straightened and your legs crossed. Open your knees as much as you can; your arms comfortably beside you or on the knees. Relax.

Breathe slowly and deeply from above through the top of your head. Bring the air down along the spine. One-two-three-in and one-two-three-out. One-two-three-in and one-two-three-out.

Create the golden light coming from the universe through the Crown chakra. Bring it down to the Heart and let it draw the path into the abyss of the universe.

Start walking the yellow brick road and observe everything you come across. After a while, you arrive at a beautiful waterfall. Sit down facing it. Imagine that you take a five-pointed star from the Heart chakra that is pale blue in colour. Put it down on the ground from your palm and enlarge it to about 6 feet in diameter. As the star is standing in front of you let it fall and envelope your astral body. You feel that the essence of the star blends with your energy and merges with your body giving you its essence. Now take a 6 pointed star that is pale gold in colour and go through the same procedure. The next is a 7 pointed indigo coloured and the last one is an 8 pointed star with white colouring to it.

When you have all the 4 stars merged with you, walk to the waterfall and stand under it. Shout out all your wishes and desires and send them to the macrocosm as a request for help.

When finished, step out of the waterfall and dry yourself in the warm sun. You feel strong, able and happy.

Walk your way back to the Heart, send the light back with thanks and come back to your earthly existence.

6. Healing the Planet

Sit down on the ground, with your back straightened and your legs crossed. Open your knees as much as you can; your arms comfortably beside you or on the knees. Relax.

Breathe slowly and deeply from above through the top of your head. Bring the air down along the spine. One-two-three-in and one-two-three-out. One-two-three-in and one-two-three-out.

Before you start healing the planet you need to cleanse and heal yourself with the 2nd meditation.

When you arrive at the expansion and the healing of the loved ones, stretch your aura further until you have the feeling of bouncing off the ground, rising to the sky and fly away as a balloon. This feeling is very beautiful however do not forget that your conscious mind is needed throughout the exercise. Your mind is in charge and takes you where you desire to go.

Look at the planet from above and find the most ailing spots. Be aware of the brainwashing media and the preconceptions we like to form. Forget them totally and only observe with your inner sight. The healing happens in the mind. Look at the suffering points. Look behind the curtain and find out the cause or the powers behind the situation. As a beginner in my school, I would not advise you to go further however it is good to look at events as a free person, without behaviour patterns, scruples, preconceptions.

The next step would be the healing itself. As everything happens in the mind and it has creative power you need to compose a picture you want to see as the result of your work. It is your responsibility to create and to believe in it. If the picture wobbles the whole outcome of your work will be a disaster. Pay attention to it.

This is the way of healing Earthlings, cities, countries, groups, individuals, mountains, rivers and seas: in one word every kind of organic energies.

When you get painfully tired you release the golden energy from your aura back to the universe slowly to land you on your feet. Then you say your thanks and come back to physical existence.

7. Visiting the Bath on Mars

There are many places in the galaxy where cleansing and healing help is available, however, I very much favour the 3rd pyramid on Mars for this exercise.

This is the only meditation in this book that requires a *merkaba* and apart from it being very good and useful, I would like to teach you the basic handling of a merkaba. Again, I am aware of the many stories about the merkaba however I am about to give you a very different view of it. Merkaba is a soul spaceship that earthlings and souls from other places use for inter-planetary travelling. Every soul has a merkaba regardless of the place it lives; so do you. However, driving the merkaba needs special training that I cannot give you here therefore I decided to offer you a ride on my own teaching vehicle that I use for students' transportation. I am also going to give you passwords to use on your journey.

Sit down on the ground, with your back straightened and your legs crossed. Open your knees as much as you can; your arms comfortably beside you or on the knees. Relax.

Breathe slowly and deeply from above through the top of your head. Bring the air down along the spine. One-two-three-in and one-two-three-out. One-two-three-in and one-two-three-out.

Bring in the golden light from above and make a pathway through your Heart centre. Start walking the path and continue until you arrive at a place where there are many stationary merkabas. You cannot and should not enter any of them apart from the one bearing a huge letter H on its sides. Walk to the door, put your right thumb on the doorknob and say Atlantis. If you follow the instruction the door would open. Sit down anywhere. You do not need to do anything for it is a shuttle for my readers who want to visit the baths on Mars.

The merkaba would drop you off at the entrance of the 3rd

pyramid. Souls would come to greet you and ask for identification. You only need to say that you come from Zsa Zsa. They will let you in to use the facilities.

Entering the building you'll be given a bathrobe and a towel with some help offered in case of need. There are many pools with different coloured liquid in them. Every pool has a sign regarding the organ it is best for. As an example, there is a pool with bottle-green coloured liquid in it, saying liver and gall bladder on its side. This bath would be good for the mentioned organs. You might want to go through all, for it will not hurt. Or you might want to choose specific ones to help you with illnesses.

You plunge into the bath and stay there as long as you desire. Think about the illness you want to have cured and imagine yourself with the result of the treatment.

When finished, walk up to the first floor where you find a relaxation area that you may use without the bath at cases for stress management. Do not forget to thank everyone there.

Change back to your own clothing and catch the shuttle down to Earth. Leave the merkaba, walk back on the path, send the light back with thanks, and return to your existence here on Earth.

Note:

All my meditations are created with the utmost care to ensure your safety throughout the practice. Please do not add or remove steps. Follow the written guidance, for my responsibility cannot cover your forgetfulness or inventions. Meditations are astral travelling when you open your energy field and without proper care, damage may occur.

Self – Sufficiency

Similarly to everything in life, self-sufficiency has a degree that mirrors the knowledge and information of the person in question.

A baby starts its first attempt to become part of the Earthly community in the womb when it moves for the first time. From that minute on real education begins. Every piece of information, advice, let it be mental or physical, would add to the road to self-sufficiency.

We never really fully understand how influential our thoughts and deeds are. These early days create the foundation of later confidence, courage and knowledge. There is a vast misconception about parenthood. Some parents treat their children as if they were porcelain dolls without understanding their functional capabilities. Although the physical body needs to be discovered, the brain is fully active from the very first moment. Like a sponge, it takes in every word and emotional energy, stores them to be used at a later stage when the functions of the body are learned and time arrives for implementation. Parents should not be slaves or servants to their children, but patient teachers and guides. This is not an easy task, especially if the degree of self-sufficiency of the parents is low. A good teacher doesn't solve the equation but leads students to the solution by explaining each step on the way. It is not enough to say: *don't do this and don't do that*, but to give importance to the questions such as *why, when, where and how*. The biggest problem arises from the fact that most parents are not self-sufficient enough to go through the teaching required.

The first and very essential step in parenting is to treat your children as equals. They should have duties and chores, also time to relax and have fun. Let them know that life is happy and it needs to be lived and experienced. How many times are hear the sentence: "Why cannot you do better at school, when you have nothing else to do but study! I do everything for you! I work day and night for you!" Parents are forgetful. They do not remember the days they skipped school for some fun and enjoyment. I call it the most popular blackmail in the children-parents relationship. Naturally, it works vice versa.

The only way to reach self-sufficiency is to try yourself in different situations and learn to solve tasks that are obstacles on your path. Within the interrelations of energies, we need to provide this possibility for each other by minding our own business, bringing solutions to tasks related to our personal existence and only advise solutions to others when asked. It is very naïve to think that a wise person learns from the mistakes of others. Experience is needed to develop and maintain self-sufficiency.

As I explained earlier, the degree of self-sufficiency depends on the code brought forward from the family, one's self-confidence, eagerness to succeed, curiosity and the ability to be happy without relying on specific persons financially, emotionally or mentally.

When talking about self-sufficiency we usually mean financial independence.

Self-sufficiency is the ability to live independently. To have personal aims not related to the success of specific persons. To make decisions do not mirror the viewpoint of others and faithfully follow the desire of the Self. It is not about financial independence really. Unless you need to give yourself or the part of you up for the material support you receive, money is only a kind of energy we need to survive in the wilderness of living.

Self-sufficiency means that you are conscious of your deeds and thoughts. You have your personal aims, your ever-changeable views and strong enough to make decisions at all times.

Afterword – The Secret

I promise that I am not going to talk about anything remotely related to popular books bearing the same title. For me, it is natural that if you want something very much you would have a better chance of getting it. The more you want it the more thought forms you allocate in your brain to support your quest. Your utmost trust and belief are required as well as 100% of your focus. There isn't any room for plan B or C created by insecurity or fear. However, it only provides you with a better chance; without the main ingredient, you will never get there. This important component is *work*. Without it, your wishes will remain idle thoughts with no substance to fall back on. On the other hand, when you start working towards your goal the whole universe joins in to help. There is another important issue one needs to look at which is *possibility*. If at the age of 45 you decide to become a prima ballerina with 100% focus, no B plan and no C plan to weaken the project and you actually go to ballet classes 4 hours a day, it would never give you the result you hope for. Or wanting the latest Mercedes without having the means to finance it, your dream will be a waste of time. With many years of hard work, you might be able to save up the money, depending on your work and lifestyle. My saddest example is the many hungry children at certain places on the planet. Nobody would want food more, and unfortunately, the wish is not enough to feed starving nations.

I've almost forgotten my very favourite *laws of attraction* project, the *miracle box*. When one puts the wish into this box and waits for the result without lifting a finger...

It is not the kind of secret I want to talk about. My subject is the hidden essence of life. Now I am going to start somewhere hoping that I arrive at the conclusion needed for the understanding of my theory.

As I mentioned earlier, souls come down to Earth for experience and a healthy push with their evolution. Earth school is unique due to the physical body we need to *wear* here. This body is the tool we have to learn. It is interesting to observe new souls how much more difficult for them to learn the usage of the physical body. They start walking and talking at a far later stage than old souls did, for they do not have previous lives to remotely remember. Everything that is connected to the body needs to be learned from scratch. Walking, talking, eating, drinking, digesting, breathing, thinking, feeling and all sexual activities come as an experience to the newcomers.

I need to get back to the idea that everything is interrelated and as the consequence, everything follows the same structure. It is the pyramid, the 3-dimensional triangle that moves on a spiral created by the Flower of Life motion.

However, it is not the Flower of Life itself. The formation of life cannot be but 4-dimensional, being always connected to the universe simply because Earth and everything on it comes from there and goes back there. We are part of the whole and the whole is part of us. This view is a necessity when we really want to think holistically. While the Flower of Life is an extraordinary 2-dimensional symbol of multiplication, the pyramids follow the order of the numerological, mathematical and geometrical requirements.

It is also important to understand that the constant argument of the 2 poles that exist in everything provides the motion in organic and non-organic energies equally. The faster the motion the livelier the energy is. It works similarly to a relationship. We aim for harmony and when we arrive there the relationship loses its bite and livelihood. Due to the similarity in behaviour patterns, it becomes a one pole state where there is no ingredients to provide the motion needed. By slowing yourself down you add to the motion changes of the universe.

Females are totally confused where identity is concerned. It is not only about individual characteristics but a misunderstanding of the gender itself. Either society admits it or not this gender has been reduced to a physical–body–making machinery that searches for the perfect male to procreate with. They think about it as the only solution to happiness and the fulfilment of life. From a tender age, females are set to fantasize about the ending of their own fairy tale that changes according to the availability and events. It is all right to have a bumpy start, it might even be healthier to put the lovers through certain trials however for females the test is the waiting they have to go through. It is an idle expectancy for the perfect male to knock on the door, get married to and live happily ever after, naturally with few offspring added to the happy nucleus. The time spent in this state is definitely wasted. The longer it becomes the sadder it would be in direct ratio with the storyline. While the expectations of the surrounding grow, the self-confidence of the female in question diminishes. She becomes the centre of unhappiness for the gender, where she is required to take the responsibility for furthering the lives of females around. The mother, who doesn't know what to do with herself now that her children grew up, she wants grandchildren to carry on with mothering and fulfilling the secret desire of inducing certain behaviour patterns into the lives of the grandchildren she failed with her daughter. Sisters and friends are also putting pressure on her; some for the excitement or event, and others to see her in the same situation where they are. Usually miserable.

One might say that we only follow Darwin's evolutionary pattern however, it is an exhausted possibility finding no link between human beings and other types of DNA.

Coming back to female behaviour patterns we can observe how it changes in the presence of a male. Regardless of who the male is, a boyfriend, a lover, somebody else's boyfriend or lover, females cannot stop looking at them as a potential male with a possibility to fulfil the requirements of the mass consciousness. A pole shift in performance appears putting emphasis only on the wild or the gently innocent side of one's naturalistic in order to turn the head of the candidate. This false behaviour pattern causes quite a lot of trouble later on if the operation becomes successful. Keeping one side alive is very tiring and difficult however it becomes easier by time until the opposite fades into the background and totally diminishes the possibility to evolve.

I have mentioned earlier that everything and everybody has 2 poles as one would not exist without the other. Light only has meaning with dark and hot comes to life with cold. However, the degree of the opposites would depend on the experience of the individual. People living in Salvador de Bahia in the Northern part of Brazil would consider +15° very cold indeed while others living in La Paz Bolivia would find the same temperature very agreeable. Nevertheless, with previous experience on the Siberian winter, the same earthling in Brazil would jump to the sky with joy at the same temperature.

The opposites exist within make up a total of 100% each at every given moment. However the degree of the poles alters with the amount of experience so does the depth of emotional openness, the sharpness of the senses and with them the quality of life.

I understand that it is very contradictory to the *and lived happily ever after* for we put conditions on happiness rather than live it. As a consequence, life is a chain of Catch 22 events. It is our decision to keep circulating within the chain or find the weakest link to break out and let the fresh air in.

The common requirements for females are always harsher than for males. Females should be withdrawn and without much sexual experience, on the other hand, good mothers, lovers and housewives. On top of all, having a well-paid job is an advantage.

The situation is not better with the male counterpart. While the girls are fulfilling the expectations of the mothers, the boys are fulfilling the dreams of the mothers. They are pushed towards professions appealing to the mother, those she would have liked for her husband to have. Choices that make her proud. Have you noticed that mothers are usually prouder of their sons than daughters? From day one a mother treats her son differently. She looks at him as if he was the prince on a white horse she could never have but now, she has the opportunity to love and cherish. He is the male that belongs to her forever. The father would fade into the background and the relationship goes through a rocky stage and usually never recovers. It is also interesting to observe that divorcees with sons would usually end up alone due to the lack of interest while those with daughters do not give up the search easily.

The father–daughter relationship is a bit different. Since mothers give birth to daughters there is a certain bond between the 2 individuals. It usually changes with time for they both fight for the same thing. Then the father would step forward as the centre of attention.

I could go on and on about the difference between the female and the male behaviour pattern, for it mirrors the universe therefore everything follows the same path; however, I want to talk about the core of the matter; The Secret.

It is in the brain and deeply connected to sexuality. In the case of a male, the sexual centre is next to the seeing centre. As you remember from previous chapters apart from seeing the eye incorporates the work of the tongue as the tool of tasting, the skin for touching, the ears of hearing and the brain as the place for thinking.

The female sexual centre is next to the hearing centre that would include the tongue as the instrument of tasting and the skin responsible for touching.

Let us look at the consequences of the difference regarding sexual behaviour. The main instruments of sexual arousal for a male are his eyes. As the degree of the 2 poles, he might prefer to see everything or he is a brave hunter and would choose the hidden treasure. I do not want to elaborate on the difference between the sexual qualities of the 2 behaviour patterns - I am certain you would be able to figure it out.

As the seeing centre includes four more senses the 100% allocated for it would be divided between them: giving the eyes the biggest bulk and divide the rest between the others. The eye receives the vibration of the light reflected on the object and never the reality however vague it might be. The information received is put through a screening filter of the conscious and subconscious letting in only what is allowed by the evolutionary state of its owner. Therefore, it is safe to say that the vision would only touch some aspects of the surface without allowing for depth.

In the case of a female, only two additional senses are involved. In her case, the ruling centre is the ears where the sound causing sexual arousal comes through. Regardless of what the male says he usually gets to the point if he is clever enough to keep talking.

There is one more and definitely vital difference between the sexual behaviour patterns of the 2 poles. While in the case of a male the roles of the additional senses are divided near equally, in the case of the female thinking grabs the largest percentage leaving taste and touch on the side road.

Without having the *know-how* thinking is very dangerous indeed. It only involves the conscious, the earthly experience that proves very limited when decision making involved. Thoughts can get easily entangled and support each other without a proper reason behind. A female always has an idea to chew on and get deeper and deeper into it until loses herself in the details.

Today earthlings do not look at relationships as challenges but as a social necessity.

For a successful evolution, both poles are needed to have friction, the emotional fight to provide the motion life needs. Instead of getting to know the Self and Others, they set upon using manipulation and emotional blackmail in order to bring the 2 poles nearer to each other regarding behaviour patterns. This deed would never result in true changes only in oppression.

Yesterday I was teaching AKIA-Khem and I sent my students up to the Thunder, we usually visit on Vodoun courses, and asked them to bring thoughts about the interrelation of the 2 poles. One of them, called *I Like* came back with a very exciting view. She said that the 2 genders are like the 4 sides of the obelisk. The parallel sides belong to the same gender. Let us call them male and female sides. The male and female sides never run on the same course. They follow an individual pattern however they meet on the edge and make up a straight line. When lines get crooked the system collapses. And she went on saying that the 2 genders are like water and air. Although there is air in the water and water in the air they have the boundary of the water's surface between them. I found this description really beautiful. Thank you very much, my beautiful students!

As you can see all this upheaval is the result of one's relation to sex. Everything about the person shows in his/her approach to sexuality. It mirrors his/her way of thinking, approach to life and the universe, evolutionary stage, past lives, present life, social background, education, emotional state and illnesses.

So you see, everything revolves around sex! The whole life is sex! With the interrelation the universe is sex! It is the highest frequency energy an earthling is able to produce or come across. It is the elixir of life. I am not talking about intercourse. I am talking about the beauty of understanding the Self, the feeling of Oneness, the wonders of Nature and being part of it, the satisfying power of creation and the moment when one day you start feeling the everlasting arousal of Existence.

Have a wonderful Life!

Live the present!

www.zsazsatudos.com

zsazsa@zsazsatudos.com

Other books from the author:

- **Emotion the Machinery of Life** – The Missing Factors of Happy Relationships

- **Heavenly nourishment** – Conscious eating in 7 steps

- **Siblings** – As above so below

- **Siblings** – And they work together

- **Siblings** – Pandemic the story of mankind

Conscious togetherness – A Love Affair

- **The 4th Way** – Teaching the Gnostic Wisdom of AKIA Philosophy

- **Life is Yours to Win** – It All Happens in the Mind

- **Dancing with the Desertwolf** – Life my Eternal Love

- **The Five Minutes Man and the Girl who Fell in Love with Mint**

Thank you for leaving a review!

All the wonders!